ENCYCLOPEDIA OF
GERBILS

DAVID ROBINSON

Title page: A white gerbil and a normal gerbil. Photo by Ray Hanson.

Cover photo by Dr. Herbert R. Axelrod.

ISBN 0-87666-915-1

H-974

Distributed in the U.S. by T.F.H. Publications, Inc., 211 West Sylvania Avenue, PO Box 427, Neptune, NJ 07753; in England by T.F.H. (Gt. Britain) Ltd., 13 Nutley Lane, Reigate, Surrey; in Canada to the book store and library trade by Beaverbooks Ltd., 150 Lesmill Road, Don Mills, Ontario M38 2T5, Canada; in Canada to the pet trade by Rolf C. Hagen Ltd., 3225 Sartelon Street, Montreal 382, Quebec; in Southeast Asia by Y.W. Ong, 9 Lorong 36 Geylang, Singapore 14; in Australia and the South Pacific by Pet Imports Pty. Ltd., P.O. Box 149, Brookvale 2100, N.S.W. Australia; in South Africa by Valid Agencies, P.O. Box 51901, Randburg 2125 South Africa. Published by T.F.H. Publications, Inc., Ltd, the British Crown Colony of Hong Kong.

Contents

The features of the head and legs are recognizable in this close-up photo of a Mongolian gerbil. Photo by Dr. H.R. Axelrod.

Foreword

The pressures of modern life have a profound effect upon the animals that are kept as pets. In order to retain their popularity the modern pet has to be very adaptable, reasonably clean and easy to maintain in good health. Perhaps most important of all, it has to be housed in the minimum of space. Gerbils possess all of these assets and a good many others in addition. Generally, they are friendly little creatures that are easily tamed and controlled. Feeding requirements are simple. In the wild state, the gerbil can spare very little in the way of natural waste, making cleaning a good deal easier.

In its natural habitat the Mongolian gerbil lives in simply constructed burrows. Being a desert animal, it is used in scientific researches, especially in those related to the importance of water to survival.

It would, therefore, seem that the gerbil is the perfect pet. If this is so, why then was it not discovered earlier? This is not an easy question to answer, but the fact that most gerbil species were not discovered until the 20th century will no doubt have a great bearing on the matter. The first species to be sold in pet stores the world over was the Mongolian gerbil, and it has become so popular that when the word gerbil is mentioned it is accepted that the animal in question is the Mongolian species. There are, of course, other species of gerbil that can be kept in captivity, but they are not so endearing in their ways as the former.

Since the early days of gerbil breeding, great headway has been made in the development of new colors. This has been brought about by the intricate breeding systems practiced by leading geneticists in both medical research and animal research laboratories. Breeding gerbils for exhibition purposes has been brought to its highest degree of artfulness in England, where special rules are laid down referring to the type, coloring and general appearance of gerbils put on show.

This book has been written with the pet gerbil keeper in mind, but the finer aspects of gerbil breeding are also covered to give the layman the opportunity to discover the full delights of gerbil management and husbandry. There have been a number of small booklets published on the gerbil; although they are very good as introductory publications, they do not really go into the subject thoroughly. It is hoped that this book will provide all the information available to ensure that newcomers and established breeders will have all the answers to their questions close at hand.

Rodents in General

People—especially pet-loving people—might find it objectionable to think of such an affectionately regarded creature as the gerbil as a rodent, because people in general don't think too kindly of rodents in general. When they think of rodents they think almost immediately of rats and disease and food-stealing and sneakiness and the beady little eyes and horrible high-pitched squeals and altogether nasty death at the hand of relentless, cruel, ugly animals. But there is no way out: the gerbil is a rodent. It's not a ratty rodent or a sneaky rodent or a disease-spreading rodent or an ugly rodent (it is, rather, an attractive, useful, friendly animal)—but it's a rodent.

Taxonomists group within the order Rodentia (a large order comprising approximately 40 per cent of the mammals) porcupines, guinea pigs, moles, squirrels, woodchucks, gophers, etc., to name some of the more commonly known members. Rodents differ widely in appearance and distribution, but they share the characteristic that their teeth grow throughout life. To further differentiate the members of Rodentia, taxonomists divide the order into families, and these families are further subdivided into genera and species. For instance, gerbils are members of the family Cricetidae. Included in this family are, among others, hamsters, voles, lemmings, aquatic rats and certain New World rats. There are 32 other families besides the family Cricetidae in the order Rodentia, and each is subdivided into at least one genus and species.

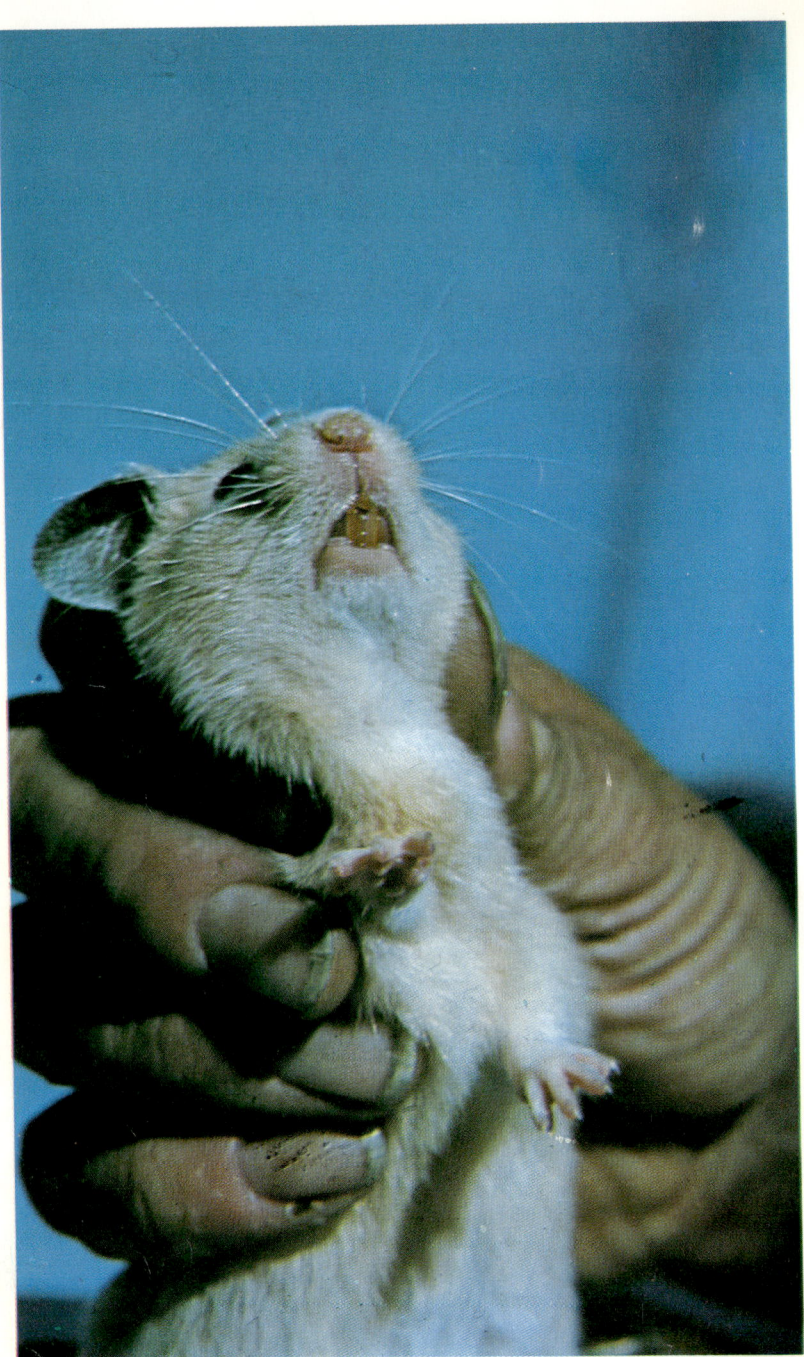

If for whatever reason the incisors of a rodent are not kept worn down in feeding, they can become excessively long, as seen in this Kenya mole rat.

Frontal view of a typical rodent, showing the upper pair of incisors; the lower incisors are concealed underneath. Photo by R. Hanson.

Thus, mice are members of the family Muridae but are cousins of the gerbil (family Cricetidae), as both are rodents. The use of genus and species may be confusing, but you can just think of these groupings as further subdivisions of the family. For example, all of the animals within a family are closely related because of their basic physical similarities, but the animals within any given genus are more closely related to each other than to animals in a different genus.

In the family Cricetidae there are several genera of rodents loosely known as gerbils, and these genera are further subdivided into species. Thus the pygmy gerbil is in the genus *Gerbillus* with 53 other species, and the Mongolian gerbil, which is the principal subject of this book, is a member of the genus *Meriones*, of which there are 12 species. Please bear in mind that the number of genera and species varies from taxonomist to taxonomist and from time to time; not everyone is of the same opinion, and opinions are subject to change.

One of the distinguishing characteristics of rodents is their teeth. The incisor teeth (the frontal ones used for cutting) grow throughout life. These teeth are continuously pushing upward from the jaw, and rodents constantly gnaw and nibble. By constantly gnawing, the rodent keeps its incisor teeth in proper condition by wearing down the enamel, or outer layer. If the teeth were not worn down they would grow past one another until they pierced the roof of the mouth. This continual grinding also leaves a peculiar pattern on the surface.

Gnawing has given the rodent a bad name, but it is only restricted to those that live in close proximity to man. Rats, for instance, have been known to eat through power lines, electrocuting themselves in the process. In other parts of the world, two members of the family Rhizomyidae cause widespread damage. In Africa the African mole has been known to cripple

Shown is a sample of materials (note the metal tubing) that has resulted from the gnawing activity of gerbils. Photo by D.G. Robinson, Jr.

horses because of the holes it digs, and in the Far East the bamboo rat will literally eat the natives out of house and home—though here, the natives get even and trap them for food. Even some gerbil species can be pests. For example, an animal known as the great gerbil is well known in the USSR for damaging crops and eating away railway embankments. (The Russians get. even and trap them for their skins.) The great gerbil is not in the same genus as our common pet gerbil.

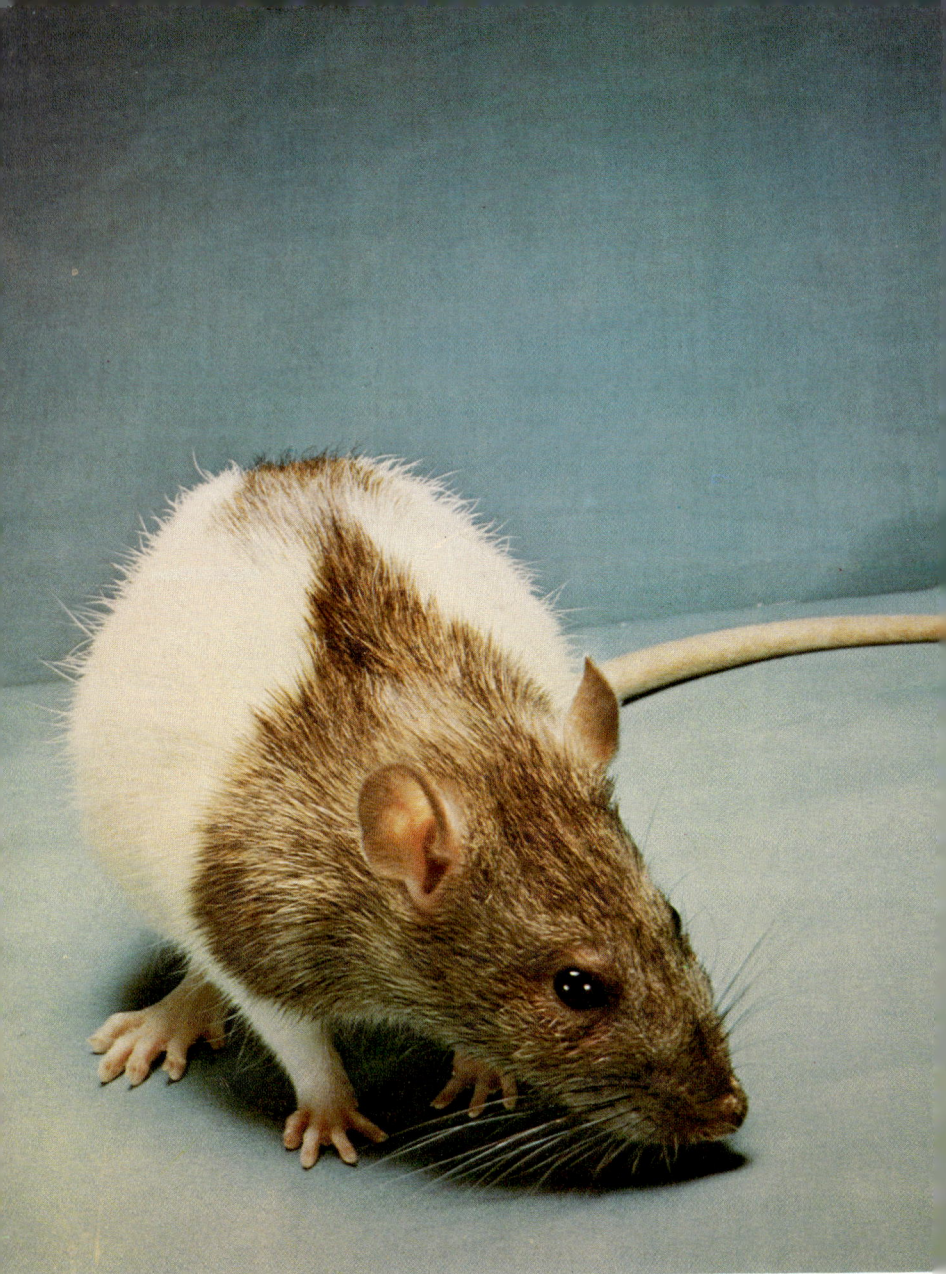

Rodents walk flat on their feet, as seen in this picture of a brown hooded rat. Five digits are recognizable in both the forelimbs and hind limbs. The thumb, is however, reduced. Photo by Dr. Herbert R. Axelrod.

Many of the rodents like this king gerbil *(Tatera boehmi)* and the red squirrel (lower photo) can stand on their hind feet, thus leaving the forelimbs free for feeding.

Despite their bad reputation, rodents are of great importance. Many destroy harmful insects and weeds. They also are widely used for laboratory experimentation. Because they have such a high birth rate and occupy such a wide area, they are a prime food source for predators, especially in the desert and semi-arid regions where they may become the sole diet.

Rodents walk on the entire foot or hand, which usually has five fingers, although the thumb may be absent. Many have internal and external cheek pouches. Those that have external cheek pouches have fur lining the inside; they can turn these inside out to clean them.

In some rodents, the tail breaks off readily, an evolutionary trait of some importance for survival. When the tail breaks off, part of it will grow back, for the tail is used as a balance with the hind feet for standing upright. In males the penis contains a baculum, which is a small bone.

CRICETIDAE—THE GERBIL FAMILY

The family Cricetidae is a big one, containing over 100 genera. Its range is world-wide except for certain islands, such as Iceland, and the area around and including Australia. Included in this family is the puna mouse, which is a single species, and found in the high elevations of Peru. There are other mammals present at this altitude (4,500 to over 5,000 meters), but the puna mouse (*Punomys lemminus*) is the only known mammal that lives its entire life at these elevations. Not much is known of these mice, but they are not afraid of man and in the wild will allow themselves to be picked up.

The size of cricetid rodents is variable, from the tiny pygmy mouse (*Baiomys taylori*), which measures a scant 50 to 80 mm with a tail roughly the same size, to the muskrat, which measures 800 mm. Though gerbil species are found only in Asia, Africa and parts of

Muskrats are large rodents that live in swamps, bogs, lakes and marshes. They are sometimes trapped for their fur. Photo courtesy of the American Museum of Natural History.

Europe, there are about 53 genera of cricetids that are found only in the New World, as far north as Alaska and as far south as Patagonia. Some New World cricetids are little known, for they inhabit the densest jungles. The Central American water mouse is an example; it is also called a fishing rat, and its length is about 105 mm for the head and body, and about the same or a little shorter for the tail. The webs and toes of the feet have bristles, and the ears are almost hidden. Another little known New World member of the Cricetidae is the aquatic rat, which eats fish. It is smaller than the Central American water mouse, being about 95 mm long, with a tail longer than its body length. Specific habits and reproduction are almost unknown.

Other very small rodents, like this pencil-tailed tree mouse of Malaysia, find the narrow hollows of bamboo a safe dwelling place. It will be difficult for larger predators to pursue these small and mainly nocturnal mice into such a protected habit.

The harvest mouse is one of the smallest mammals known. Including the tail it measures only about 10 cm. The Old World harvest mouse, unlike the American harvest mice, has a prehensile tail.

The family Cricetidae also contains the lemmings, whose mass migrations to the sea are widely known. Actually there are several different genera of lemming, some of which, like the collared lemming, do not migrate at all. The lemming most widely known is the true lemming (genus *Lemmus*). There are four species in this genus, and of the four it is the Norway lemming *(L. lemmus)* which migrates to its destruction. The Norway lemming rapidly increases in number, especially when there is an ample food supply. When their numbers are too great to exist in the same area, these lemmings will migrate with a singleness of purpose believed by many people to be unmatched among animals. They will migrate through any obstacle, be it lakes, cities or swamps. Eventually some of these lemmings reach the sea, where they plunge right in and start swimming until they drown.

Most cricetids feed solely on plant material, but some include flesh in their diet. In the warmer climates they breed all year round; the offspring of the smaller members weigh only a few grams at birth.

At least one genus of the family is thought to be extinct. This genus contained three species and was known as the West Indies giant rice rat. Only a few specimens are in the Paris Museum. These giant rice rats had a head and body length of about 360 mm and a tail length of 330 mm. They inhabited the Lesser Antilles and lived in burrows, although they took to the water when pursued. They had glands that secreted a musky substance, and they were hunted by the natives for food. They were exterminated by the European settlers because of crop damage, becoming extinct around 1900.

JERBOAS AND HETEROMYID MICE
Before continuing with gerbils, there are several other rodents that are interesting and worth learning

about because of their potential as pets. The rodents described here do not belong to the family Cricetidae. All jerboas belong to the family Dipodidae; kangaroo rats, kangaroo mice, pocket mice and spiny pocket mice all belong to the family Heteromyidae. Heteromyidae literally means "different mice"; it is a New World family containing five genera (two genera of spiny pocket mice) exhibiting a wide variety in appearance. Kangaroo rats (genus *Dipodomys*), for instance, have long, powerful hind legs which they use for jumping like the jerboa; pocket mice (genus *Perognathus*) look much like regular house mice except that they are furrier and have slightly longer hind legs. Like gerbils, jerboas and heteromyid mice live in arid climates, although the pocket mouse is found in less dry areas in southern Canada and the western United States.

JERBOAS

The family Dipodidae comprises 10 genera and 25 species; translated from the Greek, the family name means "two-footed." Dipodids are found in northern Africa eastward into Asia as far as China. All members of this family are called jerboas and are characterized by their incredible jumping adaptation. The hind legs are at least four times as large as the front legs. The jerboas spend their lives standing upright on their enormous hind legs. A typical size for the body is about 100 mm in length; the hind feet will be three-quarters this size, giving the jerboa speed and a good footing on the sandy terrain in which it usually is found.

Jerboas usually live in sandy soil and have tufts of bristly hairs under the toes and soles of their feet. This aids in supporting them and gives them a kicking action when they move. They jump rather than run from predators, and when moving slowly they hop rather like rabbits. They can leap up to 3 meters when moving fast.

House mice are very prolific and can over-populate any place within a short time. The gestation period is short (21 days) and a female can mate a short while after birth. Wild mice are destructive and carry disease besides.

The albino or white mouse, a domesticated form, is bred almost like a machine for commercial and laboratory purposes. The gerbil has not yet reached the popularity of white mice and rats as a laboratory animal. Photo by Dr. Herbert R. Axelrod.

Jerboas have external cheek pouches. These are fur-lined, and the jerboa can turn them inside out to clean them.

All jerboas have large eyes. Members of the genus genus *Jaculus*, which contains four species, have a thickened fold of skin over the nose; this fold can be drawn over the nostrils for burrowing purposes. There are four species of *Jaculus* found in northern Africa, Iran and Russian Turkestan. Their common name is desert jerboas or hairy-footed jerboas.

Perhaps the most common jerboa is the greater Egyptian jerboa. It belongs to the genus *Allactaga* and is also known as the five-toed jerboa. The greater Egyptian jerboa is nocturnal and digs burrows in flat areas and salt marshes in the hills of Egypt. This jerboa is very fast; and has, in fact, been known to race side by side with cars traveling on the desert roads. The long hind legs of the jerboa are very powerful indeed; the toes and soles of the feet are covered with hair to enable them to grip the loose sand. The tail, hairless except for a stiff bushy tip, is at least as long as the jerboa's body. During a series of leaps, the tail is held parallel to the body, moving slowly up and down in the air in order to maintain balance and stability. At this time the short forefeet are tucked under the chin out of harm's way and the head is extended slightly in order to minimize wind-resistance. The jerboa relies on its great speed to escape its enemies. The burrow is shallow and has an escape or bolt hole at the rear.

During the fantastically hot summers of the Sahara Desert, temperatures rise in excess of 167°F. It is during periods of such heat that the jerboa goes into a state of unconsciousness referred to as estivation. The purposes of this condition are the same as those of winter hibernation: the body's metabolic rate is considerably slowed, and thus energy—along with valuable moisture—is conserved. During winter hibernation the same thing happens, but it is heat and body fat that are conserved. The jerboa species that inhabit the colder climates of eastern Europe actually hibernate. It is interesting to come across a creature that shows the tendency to both estivate and hibernate according to where it lives.

Not much is known about the breeding habits of jerboas. They are solitary by nature and socialize only during the breeding season of April to June. The gestation period of the jerboa is almost twice as long as that of the gerbil and the kangaroo rat, about 40 to 42 days. The young jerboas leave the nest at around six weeks of age, by which time they are quite independent of their parents.

In general, jerboas are not often kept as pets. They require special attention, but there are no real reasons why an interested owner should not keep them in captivity. Jerboas in captivity are somewhat delicate creatures. They need warmth, a varied diet and, of course, clean water to stay healthy. By far the most secure way of housing jerboas is to provide them with a strong aquarium. This, however, needs to be of a good size, or the jerboa will be too cramped. A strong lid should be fastened on the top with adequate holes drilled for ventilation. Artificial heating is best provided by a low watt lamp in a holder on the underside of the lid. To prevent the jerboa from burning itself on the lamp, make a false ceiling with a sheet of wire over which the lid can be fixed.

Jerboas are aggressive and do not take kindly to being handled. Therefore, treat them with caution and do not take unnecessary risks. Bites can be serious and if not treated properly can become inflamed and lead to trouble.

A pair of young common (Norwegian) rats that have tunneled through a discarded half loaf of bread. Rats can carry and spread epidemic diseases; a very good example is the bubonic plague of the Middle Ages, also known as Black Death.

KANGAROO RATS

There are 22 species of kangaroo rats in the genus *Dipodomys*. They are found in southwestern Canada through the western states of the United States into Mexico. Like the jerboas, kangaroo rats travel by hopping on their hind legs. They are burrowers but prefer open terrain that gives them an unobstructed view of their territory. They seldom drink water, getting their moisture from the seeds and other vegetation which they eat. They do bathe—in the dusty sand around their burrows. In fact, pets which are not kept in sand or are otherwise denied this bathing behavior develop sores on their bodies and usually develop matting of the fur. This is due to a gland on their back which secretes oil; the dust-bath apparently is a means of coagulating the oil for grooming and eventual removal. Kangaroo rats emit no noise but communicate by a method of thumping and rattling sounds with their hind legs.

Kangaroo rats are somewhat extraordinary in appearance; they have very large heads with black eyes and ears that lie flat to the head. The body is often quite large, being about five inches long. Their forelimbs are short, as with the gerbil, and they have hand-like paws. The thin and extremely long hind limbs are perhaps the most striking feature. The ankle is situated roughly halfway up the leg, which makes the actual leg rather short and the toes very extended. Both sets of limbs have long sharp nails which can inflict severe injuries on any rival. The kangaroo rat's tail constitutes half of the animal's total length. It is thin and whip-like, ending in a tuft of thick black hairs.

Many people find the kangaroo rats beautiful in comparison to other desert-dwelling rodents. The whole of the head and back are a light brown, which in some species may tend to appear gray. The underside and legs are white, and there is also a white streak along the

A kangaroo rat. Note the well developed hind limbs. Photo courtesy of the American Museum of Natural History.

A banner-tailed kangaroo rat with the characteristic bushy tip of its tail showing. Photo courtesy of the American Museum of Natural History.

Second in importance to mice as a research animal is yet another rodent, the white or albino form of the common rat (upper photo). The white rat is scarcely comparable to the wild form of rat; an undesirable quality for a research animal, aggressiveness, no longer exists.

Small mammal breeders, including gerbil breeders, strive to produce new varieties through selective breeding. Shown is an unstandardized light brown and white patterned rat. Photo by Dr. H.R. Axelrod.

Through selective breeding countless varieties of fancy or exhibition rats are now available. The hooded pattern is a popular and a stable variety.

haunches. Of the many species and subspecies of this animal, each one is rather similarly marked.

Unlike gerbils, kangaroo rats prefer to travel in leaps. They can cover distances of over six feet in one single jump. Against their traditional enemy the rattlesnake, the kangaroo rats effectively band together to harass the attacker: they encircle the snake and in turn stand boldly in front of him. As he strikes, the kangaroo rat sidesteps the lunge and flicks sand into the snake's eyes. These tactics offer distraction to a rattlesnake bent on entering the nests of the kangaroo rat and devouring the young.

Another remarkable characteristic of these creatures is their habit of storing food. Kangaroo rats have a cheek pouch on both sides of the head, and into these pouches they cram all the seeds, grasses and plants they can gather in a night's expedition. The contents are later placed in shallow ditches around the burrow. The food is lightly covered with soil and left for the sun to dry it out during the day. The next night it is removed to the permanent food store within the burrow itself.

The kangaroo rat is wholly nocturnal in its habits; it sleeps far underground all day long in burrows which can be three feet in depth and emerges at night when the desert has cooled. It often falls prey to owls, which are usually silent enough to catch it unaware.

Kangaroo rats do not form organized colonies, but they are never very far from members of their own kind. They are very solitary animals that only come into direct contact with others of their species during the breeding season. Normally, they avoid each other as much as possible, but if two rival males should meet, they may fight to the death. In fighting they use their hind legs to strike and inflict grievous injuries with the claws. Though these fights often end in death, the strange thing is that they are fought in absolute silence.

Kangaroo rats may breed in any month of the year, up to three litters being produced a year. The gestation period is about 29-33 days, at the end of which a litter of about two to four young are born. Baby kangaroo rats are born blind, deaf and quite hairless. Their limbs are very short at birth, but as the young animals start to feed, their limbs increase in length until by the time of weaning the babies are perfect miniatures of their parents.Female kangaroo rats have strong maternal instincts and have been known to remove a litter of young to a considerable distance when the nest has been disturbed.

Kangaroo rats are not difficult to keep in captivity, but they must be kept singly and not in pairs; they fight readily, and this should be avoided as much as possible. If breeding is attempted, a nest box should be provided for the female to rear her family. Kangaroo rats are shy and secretive by nature, and it rquires very patient handling to tame them. Never try to pick one up straight away; start by offering food in the hand and gradually increase the animal's confidence in you.

The two most popular kangaroo rats are the banner-tailed kangaroo rat (which is the largest of the genus and measures 14 inches including the tail) and the most common form, the dwarf kangaroo rat. When fully adult, the dwarf measures only about six inches in length.

The kangaroo rat's diet is simple: it should be based on a proprietary rodent mixture plus any edible green food. In the wild kangaroo rats seldom drink water, instead obtaining it from their food; it is a good idea to have water available for captive animals, however.

POCKET MICE

Pocket mice are members of the genus *Perognathus*, which contains 25 species. Their range is

A pair of albino hamsters. On account of the absence of pigments in the iris of the eyes, they appear pink. Hamsters are also used in research. Photo by R. Hanson.

roughly similar to that of the kangaroo rat, from southwestern Canada through the western United States into Mexico. They are not "true" mice (mice are members of the family Muridae) but hardy rodents that have evolved to inhabit some of the most barren lands in western North America. They do look like mice, but the çoat is bristly and the tail is about as long or longer than the head and body. Coloration varies on the upper parts from a pale yellow to gray; the under parts are usually white. The young pocket mice have a cute, furry coat, but as they grow older they will molt, with the characteristic bristly coat growing back in.

Their principal food is seeds and desert vegetation, though they are known to consume insects. Like the kangaroo rats they do not drink water, obtaining their moisture from the foods they eat. They also store food in their burrows. The hind limbs are not much larger than the forelimbs, and they move just like any other mouse. The forelimbs have long claws that are used for burrowing.

Pocket mice are nocturnal and during the day remain in their burrows. Their reproduction takes place from April to September, though during the hot months of June and July breeding is minimal. They make good pets, as they require hardly any care, and can be kept adequately on a steady diet of birdseed. They can live for up to six years in captivity.

SPINY POCKET MICE

There are two genera of spiny pocket mice, *Liomys* (spiny pocket mice), comprised of 11 species and *Heteromys* (forest spiny pocket mice), comprised of 10 species. The forest spiny pocket mice are very similar to their northern cousins, the principal differences being in the teeth and the cranial structure. The forest spiny pocket mice are rather rare as pets, though, because

A trio of exhibition types of mice: selfs (unpatterned coat) in blue, cream and black. Photo by H.V. Lacey.

they inhabit the tropical, wet regions of southern Mexico down through Colombia and Ecuador.

Spiny pocket mice inhabit southern Texas and Mexico down to Panama. Their coat is harsh, as their name implies. The hairs are stiff, flat and grooved, and interspersed with more flexible hairs. The tail is well haired and sometimes has more than one color. The underside is generally white, while the bristly hair on top is dark, generally grayish brown to black.

Like all heteromyid mice they eat seeds and vegetation. They have external cheek pouches that open outside the mouth and extend back to almost the shoulder area. The mouse can turn these inside out for cleaning. Another distinguishing characteristic is the presence of a small spoon-like digit on the hind foot, which is probably used for digging or grooming. Incidentally, pocket mice burrow very quickly. Their burrows are usually under rocks or bushes in the wild. Young are born during spring or early summer and number from two to four.

KANGAROO MICE

Kangaroo mice look similar to kangaroo rats but are smaller (about half as large as kangaroo rats) and move by leaping with their large hind legs. They belong to the genus *Microdipodops*. There are only two species. *M. megacephalus*, the dark kangaroo mouse, is found in southern Oregon and Utah; *M. pallidus*, the pale kangaroo mouse is found in west-central Nevada. They prefer a high elevation (1,000 to 2,000 meters) and live near shrubs near sand dunes. Kangaroo mice are gentle pets and are very sensitive to light. They are best kept in the basement or in an area without too much light or with an effective shade. They live long and, like other heteromyid mice, do not need a separate supply of water, obtaining all their moisture from the food they eat.

The dark kangaroo mouse is brown or grayish black, and the underparts are lighter. In the pale kangaroo mouse the upper parts are pale creamy buff and the underparts are as white as a rabbit's. Both species store fat in their tails, and the kangaroo mice (which are also called pygmy kangaroo rats) have very large heads, larger than those of any other heteromyid mice.

The hind feet are fringed at the sides with stiff hairs, and the undersurfaces are well furred. A full-grown mouse weighs between 10 and 16 grams. Their litters number from one to seven; there may be two in a year.

Gerbils in the Wild

Gerbils are extremely well adapted to living in desert and semi-desert conditions. The countries populated by gerbils include the whole of the northern part of Africa, spreading eastward through Arabia, Israel and Turkey, then northeastward to Mongolia and northern China. Many of the lesser-known gerbils species are very rarely seen even in the wild state, since the areas they inhabit are so desolate and inaccessible to the wildlife enthusiast. Gerbils are burrowing creatures; they spend the greater part of the hot arid day underground where they are safe from their enemies and where they can conserve their energy for the nightly food-foraging excursions.

Many of the species of gerbil are wholly nocturnal in their habits and are rarely seen in the open by daylight. The breeding habits of gerbils vary a great deal. The Mongolian gerbil, for example, will rear as many as six litters a year, while other species may restrict their breeding to a single litter. A number of the species lead a life of solitude and come into contact with members of the opposite sex only during the breeding season.

Many, but not all, species hibernate during winter. However, the fat-tailed gerbil lives in a climate where cold temperatures are not a problem. Instead, the reverse is the case; the winter months become only slightly cooler, while in summer the sun is unbearably hot. At this time, such gerbils go into a stupor similar to that of winter hibernation. Their respiration slows down and becomes shallow until activity ceases; the ger-

This burrow was built by a captive gerbil that was set free. In the desert gerbils' burrows can have multiple exits. Photo by Dr. H.R. Axelrod.

bil sleeps in this way until the cooler winter months, when it awakens and resumes normal activity.

Gerbils vary in size from two inches up to nine or ten inches long. Very often, the tail is of equal length to that of the body. Depending on the size of the species, they all resemble either a mouse or a rat in appearance. The ears are usually quite large and rounded; the skull is wide and broad and the body hunched when the animal stands on its hind feet, which are long and kangaroo-like. The forefeet are very short and have paws that resemble hands. Gerbils have elongated hind legs which provide them with a speedy mode of travel; the color of their fur is more or less uniform throughout the whole family, though some may appear reddish while others are of a more grayish hue, these differences being due to the varying climates and conditions in which they live.

In appearance all gerbils seem much the same. Their size of course varies from species to species, but an average length (not counting the tail) would be about four inches. The limbs are a very prominent feature of the anatomy, with the forepaws rather like hands which hold food during feeding. The hind feet are used in a variety of ways, the most important of which is to enable the gerbil to stand firmly on the ever-shifting sands of its desert habitat. The hind toes are elongated and form a snowshoe-like shape, with the claws being fairly long (the Mongolian gerbil is in fact referred to as the "clawed gerbil"). The gerbil's hind limbs are elongated and reminiscent of those of the kangaroo. The forelimbs are very short, although walking is usually done on all fours. The hind limbs are used when the gerbil stops and stands up to survey the horizon for any signs of danger. The tail is used for support when the animal stands. It is approximately the same length as the body, covered with hair and ending in a bushy tip. The tail is also in action when the gerbil leaps along, a mode of travel frequently seen among desert rodents. The tail acts as a rudder and stabilizer as the hind legs catapult the gerbil through the air. A gerbil in captivity will rarely jump at all.

The gerbil's head is set well into the body and in most instances is short and broad, not being at all rat-like in appearance. The eyes are large and bright, so large, in fact, that they often appear to be almost popping out of the head. Gerbils are very sharp-sighted, unlike many other rodent species, which can see only a few inches in front of them. The general color of the eye is black, but in some species they may be brown or even gray.

For a creature that relies to such an extent on its sense of hearing, the gerbil does not possess extraordinarily large ears. The secret of the gerbil's acute hearing lies within it skull. It possesses enlarged cavities termed *tympanic bullae* which act in much the same way as an amplifier and magnify the slightest sound.

In its wild habitat, the gerbil feeds on hard-cased seeds and nuts, and it needs very strong, sharp teeth to crack them open. As the gerbil gnaws, the leading edges of the upper and lower front teeth slide over each other and just touch. The result is that the soft inside is continualy worn away and leaves a very sharp edge. There are species of gerbil that possess cheek pouches, but these are the exception rather than the rule. It is also known that certain gerbils store food in their burrows, although they do not show this habit when kept in cages.

The usual color of gerbils is a reddish brown, although in individuals this color may range from yellow through shades of dark gray. The underside or belly fur is usually white but may also be cream. There are very good reasons for the color combinations, the first being a camouflage against the usual background of sand and rock. The white stomach fur acts also as a reflector of heat from the sand of the desert. Because the abdomen contains many of the vital organs, it has to be protected from the severe heat of the desert if the animal is not to suffer from dehydration.

Wild gerbils' feedings habits are naturally linked to the environment in which they live. Since food is scarce in the desert, it must be gathered when plentiful and stored for future use. The gerbil collects its food at night after the hot sands have cooled. Seeds of varying kinds are eaten, as well as stalks and even flowers of plants. Water, of course, is at a premium under harsh desert conditions and has to be conserved if the gerbil is to survive. Water, often found within roots and tubers a few inches below the surface of the sand, is stored within the gerbil's body in the form of body fat. During periods of extreme drought this internal fat is gradually used up and then replenished when the rains eventually fall.

All gerbil species live in tunnels or burrows, which they very often dig to a depth of three to four feet. Once within their tunnels, the gerbil is safe from almost any predator, be it the desert fox, hawks, owls or even—to a certain extent—man himself. Though it is often said that gerbils do not perspire, this is untrue; they do in fact sweat, but they do so only in order to maintain the humidity level within their burrows. To do this, they block the entrance hole at nighttime with sand. As the temperature rises, the gerbil sweats and so increases the humidity level. This has the effect of keeping the burrows cool. Gerbils kept in an inadequately ventilated aquarium will usualy be steamed up. The gerbil burrow may be a simple tube or catacomb of little storerooms and breeding dens, but the main tunnels for each family do not connect with each other.

Gerbils are usually not gregarious; they prefer to live with their own family only and will fight others who come too near or appear to threaten their security. The Jerusalem gerbil, one of the largest, prefers to lead a solitary life. This gerbil will mate with a female and then go its own way, having nothing to do with its family. In captivity it can become very aggressive toward anything that disturbs its peace and quiet. Species such as the Libyan and Mongolian gerbils, however, stay with their mates throughout their whole lifetime. Even after the death of one or the other, the survivor will not readily take another mate, and this characteristic is particularly noticeable when they are kept in captivity.

It is difficult to say whether gerbils actually make their nests inside the burrows. Each female will certainly have her own tunnel with a nest site at the end, and it is the number of individual tunnels which make up the community. If gerbils in captivity are not provided with nesting material, they will make no attempt to construct a nest from the bits and pieces on the cage floor. If this practice also applies in the wild state, there must be quite a number of young gerbils that do not survive to the weaning stage.

The females of most species come into estrus every five to ten days; during this period they will accept the male at any time, mating being a continual activity until the heat period passes. The usual gestation period is about 25-29 days, after which a litter of between one and ten young is born. Baby gerbils are completely naked, blind, deaf and without teeth. Growth is rapid during the first fourteen days, by which time the youngsters are covered with a soft pale brown fur. Weaning takes place around the twenty-first to the twenty-eighth day. Sometimes there are further litters of young within the nest before the previous litter has made its way into the open.

Young gerbils come into adolescence at about nine weeks of age and by their twelfth week are sexually mature. The young adults will then leave their home territory to find a mate—perhaps only a few yards away; after some quite serious fights, they will set up home either in a disused burrow or make a fresh one which in time becomes a new gerbil community.

Gerbils do not have a long span of life, the maximum age reached being about five years. This figure has been arrived at from gerbils in captivity, and it is likely that the wild gerbil does not live anywhere near as long. Many hazards face a gerbil in the wild during its lifetime, which it would not meet in captivity. Disease is rife, and it has powerful enemies such as snakes, foxes, hawks and owls to contend with.

Generally, the sounds of the gerbil's voice is limited to a series of high-pitched squeaks. These sounds are heard only when the animal is frightened or excited, as

In this stance a Mongolian gerbil is able to produce a drum-like noise by continuous stamping of the hind feet on the ground. The significance of this behavior is not fully understood. Photo by D.G. Robinson, Jr.

during fighting or mating. Young gerbils squeak while still in the nest, but after this period is over the noise is heard less and less. The Mongolian gerbil has another form of communication; we do not know whether this form can be used by all other gerbil species. When alarmed, it stands upright on its hind legs and drums with its feet. For such a small animal, the sound is very penetrating and can be heard quite a distance away. It was originally thought that this foot-stamping was a warning that danger threatened. This doesn't seem to be the case, however, because in some instances other members of the group have been observed to take up a similar stance and begin to drum also. There is now a theory that this is a way of relieving nervous tension!

The Mongolian Gerbil
in General

Of all the species of gerbil, the Mongolian gerbil is the most well-known of all. It is now so popular that it has become the common pet shop gerbil, the friendly, cheeky little creature that children love to own.

It was discovered in the early 1950's by Professor Davidson, a French zoologist well known for his finds of almost extinct species of animals from the northern regions of China, Tibet and the Himalayas; perhaps his most famous discovery was that of the giant panda, mascot of the International Wildlife Fund.

The scientific name of the Mongolian gerbil is *Meriones unguiculatus.* Meriones was a warrior in Greek mythology said to have worn a helmet adorned with tusks from a wild boar. Simply translated, *unguiculatus* is taken to mean "with fingernails" or claws.

The Mongolian gerbil was bred in captivity for the first time by Japanese scientists. In 1954, they passed some of the progeny on to Dr. Victor Schwentker of the United States. At first, gerbils were regarded as something of a curiosity, not being at all aggressive and in fact quite the opposite, inquisitive and very friendly. Their admirable qualities came to the attention of America's medical research scientists, with the result that the gerbil soon became classed as a perfect subject for laboratory work. It was, therefore, only a matter of time before it became clear that the animal would also make a very suitable pet.

GENERAL APPEARANCE

At full size (at twelve weeks of age) the Mongolian gerbil measures approximately four inches from the tip of the nose to the base of the tail. Its weight is about four ounces, males weighing slightly more than females. The male is also proportionately larger in size than his female counterpart. In appearance, both sexes appear alike, but upon closer examination, it will be seen that the male has a dark scrotal sac at the base of his tail. This sac contains all the sexual organs, contained in this way for protection: thus, the area around the base of the male's tail is somewhat enlarged. The female, on the other hand, is more rounded in this area, and the vagina and anus are close to each other.

Coloring, a reddish-brown, is the same in both sexes of the desert-dwelling rodents but lighter and darker forms are by no means rare. The extent of the dark pigmentation depends upon the amount of guard hairs contained within the coat. These hairs are always black and are heavier than the rest of the fur; they provide stiffening to the coat and protection against water. The fur is a mixture of these dark guard hairs and light brown or reddish ordinary hairs, thus giving the gerbil its distinctive appearance. Beneath the top layer of fur there is a softer and different undercoat of very dense blue-gray fur. The gerbil's underside is covered with a single thin layer of white fur that reaches as far as the chin and the forefeet. Around the ears and eyes there is a border of soft and light gray hair; the nails are black on all the toes, of which there are five on the forefeet and three on the hind feet. The gerbil's paws are very adaptable, being hand-like and used for holding food securely.

A normal and healthy looking Mongolian gerbil. The large feet and the size of the eye in relation to body size indicate its young age. Photo by D.G. Robinson, Jr.

The body is cobby and usually hunched when the gerbil squats on its elongated hind legs. In this stance, which is the normal posture, there appears to be no indication of the gerbil's neck, because of the thick-set body. The head is broad and wide; the eyes, which are usualy jet black in color, are positioned high up on the head and are beady in appearance. The ears are rounded and covered with soft light gray fur. Although the Mongolian gerbil does not have pouches, the mouth is large for such a comparatively small animal. The front teeth are beaver-like and are extremely sharp. The gerbil's short forelegs have hand-like paws that are very effective when the gerbil excavates the deep tunnels in which it makes its home.

On the underside of the belly of the adult male there is a scent gland. This gland looks like a bald patch on the belly fur; in young males it is almost unnoticeable. If the adult male wishes to leave his scent in a particular place, he slides his belly along the object and in doing so leaves his mark. The scent is undetectable to the human nose.

The long hind legs are also covered with fur and in shape resemble the hind legs of a kangaroo. The toes are so long that they take up almost two-thirds of the entire foot, which is bent at the ankle joint. The Mongolian gerbil's tail is perhaps its most important asset; it acts as a stabilizer and prop and for this purpose is thick and hair-covered. Along the entire length of the tail there is a ridge of black hairs that ends in a tuft of black hairs in much the same fashion as an artist's small paint brush. The underside of the tail is covered with light sandy hair that is sparse and fine in texture.

The skin covering the tail is loose and can easily become detached if handled roughly. When this happens, the bone structure of the tail is revealed to be a chain of nodules gradually becoming smaller as the tail tapers to a point. The fur-tufted tail is of prime importance; it helps to steady the gerbil's body as it stands on its haunches and is also used as a rudder during the animal's leaps and bounds.

The hind feet are elongated to maintain the balance a gerbil needs as it squats on its haunches. Jumping in great leaps is one of the Mongolian gerbil's showiest tricks, but this is not the way in which it normally travels. It generally moves with quick jerky movements, much in the manner of a squirrel. All four feet are in action in this method for walking, though the gerbil never moves far without standing on its hind legs to scan the horizon. Gerbils that are born and bred in captivity do not jump without cause; even when they are made to jump, a distance of only eighteen inches horizontally and six inches vertically is the normal maximum. Young gerbils that are nervous or frightened will leap in any direction if they are startled by a quick movement or a loud noise; however, taming and patient handling will soon overcome this nervousness.

The Mongolian gerbil cannot really be described as rat-like or mouse-like, since its head is comparatively much broader. The ears are tulip-shaped and covered with hair, the bold black eyes placed high on each side of the skull.

REPRODUCTION IN THE WILD

Burrowing is second nature to a gerbil, and it is in this way that wild gerbils excavate the long dark tunnels that are their homes. These tunnels are often interconnecting, because the Mongolian gerbil is gregarious and—in the wild, at least—will live in complete harmony with its fellows.

There is no distinct breeding season, since the gerbil will breed at any time during the warmer months of the year. Once a pair of Mongolian gerbils have mated

A litter of young gerbils in various attitudes ranging from sheer nonchalance to extreme curiosity. Photo by D.G. Robinson, Jr.

they are inseparable, the pair-bonding being so strong that if one or the other should die, the remaining partner is very reluctant to accept another mate. The female gerbil comes into estrus once a week, the season or period of receptiveness lasting a few hours. During this time, the male constantly pursues his mate, almost never leaving her alone. The acts of copulation last only a matter of a few seconds; after each, the male washes himself and then returns to continue his attentions. This is one of the few times that the gerbil will be heard to utter its shrill squeak. The gestation period of the Mongolian gerbil lasts about 24 days; during the early stages, the female does not show any signs that she is expecting a litter. After the 20th day, however, her body swells alarmingly until it seems as though she would burst. The litter will number anywhere from a single youngster up to ten.

To give birth, the female gerbil stands on her hind legs and reaches down with her mouth to pull the newborn young from her. All placentas and any dead young are quickly eaten in the cleaning process. Young Mongolian gerbils are born blind, deaf and quite hairless. Within a matter of two or three hours after birth, the skin of the babies starts to take on a dark hue as pigmentation begins to show beneath the surface. During their first week of life, young gerbils are very active as they grope their way around the nest; their voices are also loud as they fight for position around their mother. They also become progressively darker as their hair makes its way to the surface of the skin. Their eyes and ears are still tightly closed, however, and remain like this until the young gerbils are ten days old. The ears are the first to open, and then the short limbs and tail begins to lengthen. From the moment the young gerbils are born, the male of the pair assumes his parental duties: he sits on the litter while the female takes

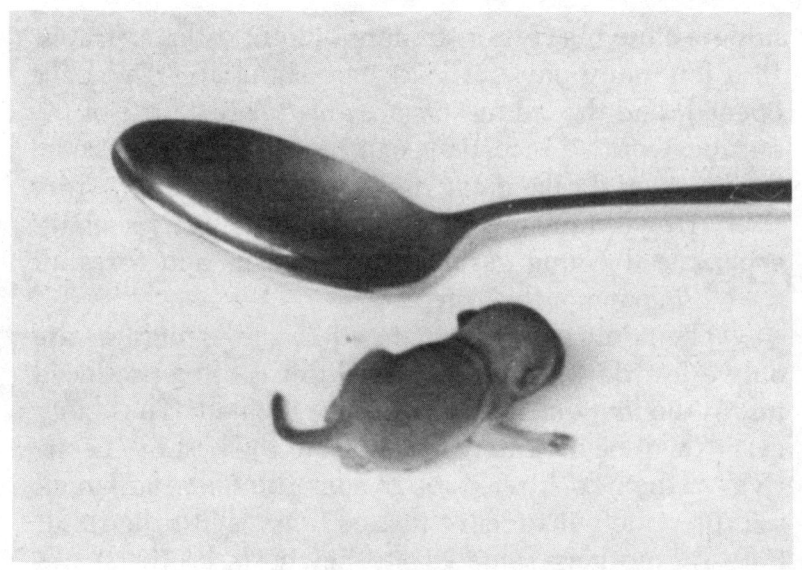

At the age of three days a gerbil is very helpless, like most other mammals. It is so small that it can be carried on a spoon.

time off to find food for herself. The male cannot by any means be called the perfect father, but he perseveres with the wriggling babies as long as the female is away and the nest needs protection.

By the tenth day, the young gerbils have a light covering of golden brown fur. At this stage, their ears will have opened, and although they are still quite blind, they can hear perfectly. By the time the babies are about seventeen days of age, their incisor teeth will have developed, and the young are not so dependent upon their mother, since at this stage, they are crawling around on weak legs, blindly exploring the nooks and crannies of their underground nursery. They find food that has been lying about and, in so doing, soon wean themselves. As they grow stronger, the babies become a real handful for their parents as they scramble to the entrance of the burrow. No doubt the attraction of the light outside spurs them on, since even though the eyelids are closed, a certain amount of light still penetrates. In a few more days, at least one of the eyes will have opened, and the youngsters are able to see a little of the outside world. Once they can see well, they become foolhardy and take great risks by venturing away from the burrow. Many predators are on the alert for such inexperienced young gerbils; owls, snakes and foxes all have hungry mouths to feed.

The adult pair will mate while the youngsters are only a few days old, so another litter is often produced just as the first one is about to leave the nest. The young gerbils will be definitely ousted from the nest by the arrival of the next litter, though sometimes an individual will be reluctant to leave its sanctuary, with the result that it smothers some of its newborn brothers and sisters. The survival rate in captivity is estimated at about fifty per cent; in the wild, this percentage is much reduced and could even come as low as twenty per cent.

After the young gerbil leaves the nest, its growth rate slows down considerably, and food intake begins to level off.

The youngsters never venture far from the place where they were born. This is the way that the gerbil community forms itself, because as the young adults nest nearby and are followed by further generations, their population gradually builds up. Overcrowding does not seem a serious problem to wild gerbils, because natural mortality factors keep the population in check. At nine weeks of age, sexual maturity is reached, and pairs soon form the bond that will bind them for the rest of their breeding lives—a year to a year and a half.

Making Friends
with Gerbils

The relationship that exists between the gerbil keeper and his gerbils depends entirely upon the kind of attitude he takes toward his charges. A negative approach can never lay the foundations for firm friendship and understanding. It will only breed contempt which may in turn change to hate.

The greatest motivator in the animal world is fear, and fear can make the most docile gerbil into an

Direct contact with gerbils should start early to familiarize them with your touch and voice. Photo by Dr. H.R. Axelrod.

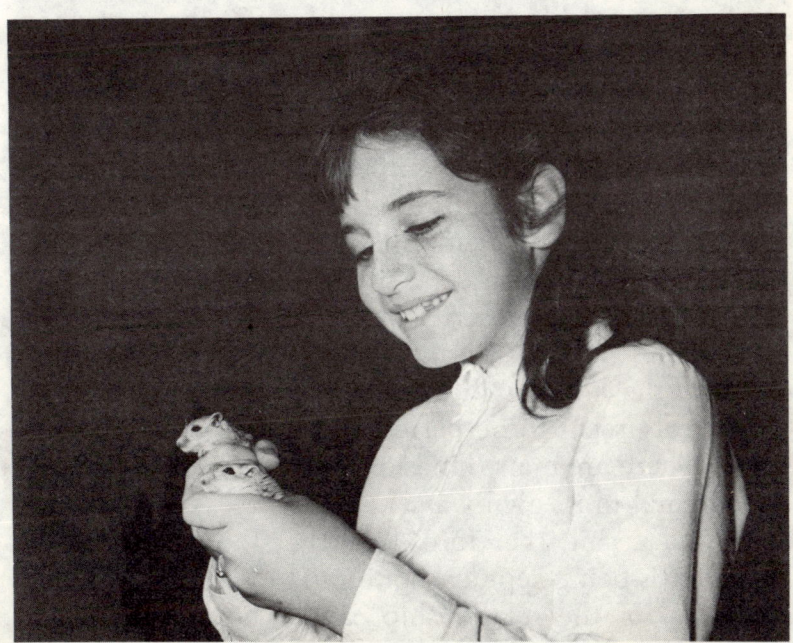

unmanageable wild animal. There have been many experiments to try to find the reason for an animal's instinctive fear of humans. Animals that appear perfectly at ease in the company of humans and are provided with every amenity will very often refuse to breed. Attempts to breed from rare and almost extinct species are often made in the world's zoos, the idea behind the attempts being that once the number of captive-bred animals reaches a satisfactory level, the surplus can then be reintroduced into the wild state to try to replenish the depleted number of animals naturally existing in the wild. In most cases, the experiments have ended in total failure, although there are some notable exceptions. These exceptions are mostly concerned with animals that once roamed wild over western Europe. The European wolf, for instance, was once widespread over this area but now lives in tiny pockets of northern Italy. In Germany, the wolves have been encouraged to breed in compounds that are fully protected from hunters. They lead a normal life but are strictly under the control of man. The European eagle owl has been bred in huge aviaries, and the young birds have been set free into the surrounding forests. The European bison has also been bred in this way, and the same success has been achieved. The American bison, too, is to the point that there now is a surplus of them, and their breeders are trying to find ways to make the animals economically useful. The conclusion reached from the failures is that the animals have been suffering from stress, a condition that renders the animals ill at ease even though they may outwardly seem to be perfectly satisfied with life in a cage. There are many kinds of stress, each one affecting the animal in its own way.

If a gerbil, therefore, feels that the conditions in which it is being kept are not quite to its liking, the full potential of the relationship cannot be reached. The

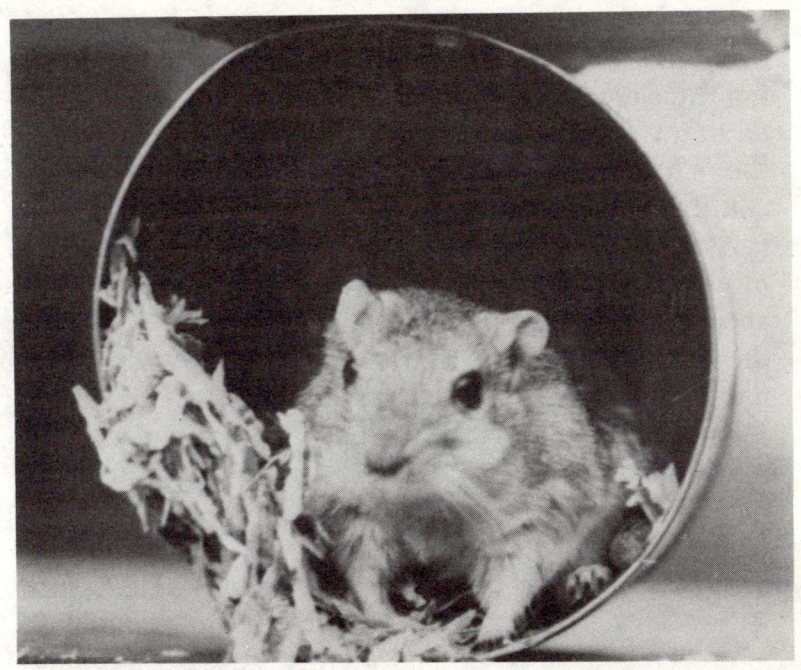

The feeling of security offered by an ordinary tin can to this home-bred gerbil is comparable to a burrow to a wild gerbil in its desert habitat.

gerbil may even be encouraged to breed, but it will do so only spasmodically and not to a regular pattern. Fortunately, rodents in general are renowned for their capacity to accept the confines of a cage. Even in the wild state, rodents will quickly settle down to a life that is affected by the presence of man. The rat and mouse are classic examples of animals that have learned to adapt themselves to a life that depends to a great extent upon the close proximity of humans. When gerbils were first encountered in the wild, their disregard for man was apparent. They were found to be quite unafraid of the approach of human footsteps. Wild gerbils actually came out of their burrows to get a good look at the strange two-legged creatures that ventured into their territory.

The person who has never owned a pet before could not do better than to start with a gerbil. By keeping these creatures, a first-class knowledge can be gained in the ways of animals. Gerbils are very valuable in the education of young or mentally sub-developed children; much can be taught simply by keeping some gerbils within the school room. Children learn much more quickly by practice than by theory and should be encouraged to take part in the daily routine of tending the gerbils. In this way, they project themselves into part of the gerbils' life and accept also the enlarging responsibility of making sure that the gerbils are properly housed and fed.

OBTAINING YOUR FIRST GERBIL

To ensure that the prospective gerbil-keeper begins with a suitable animal, it is of prime importance that the gerbil be healthy and normal. It is no use to try and tame a gerbil that is ill or that has been mistreated and is therefore suspicious of its handler.

In choosing your gerbil, look at its fur. The state of the coat is a very good guide to its general condition. It should be clean and even, should have no bare patches and should not come away when pulled. A good sheen on the coat is desirable, but this may be difficult to see in a bad light. The belly fur is equally as important; it too should be clean and smooth. There should be no sores or cuts anywhere on the body, which includes the tail. Some gerbils may have been unfortunate enough to have lost part of their tail. This can be the result of a number of things, the most common of which is that the gerbil has been provided with an exercise wheel. These are dangerous where gerbils are concerned. The gerbil's tail cannot be kept out of the way while the gerbil is running around inside the wheel. Although a gerbil with a shortened tail is not at much disadvantage, he

Unless too young or too ill, gerbils can generally withstand much handling (barring deliberate maltreatment) even by children.

An adequate set-up for keeping a few gerbils, except for the exercise wheel, which can be dangerous to gerbils. Photo by Dr. H.R. Axelrod.

has lost a great deal of elegance! Fighting can sometimes be a reason for cuts along the tail; fortunately, such cuts usually heal without trouble.

Pay particular attention to the eyes; they should be clear and bright. The presence of water or foreign matter in them may simply mean the gerbil has a cold. Watery eyes can also be caused by drafts. If these simple guidelines are followed, there is a good chance that the chosen gerbil will be thoroughly sound.

Obvious physical signs of ill health are not the only thing you should look for. Sick gerbils *act* sick, and it is not difficult to distinguish between a healthy, robust gerbil and one that is unwell. First, look at what the gerbil is doing while it is in the cage. If it is in the company of others, it may very well be asleep, but on your approach the gerbils should wake up and come to the front of the cage in order to investigate the disturbance. A fit, healthy gerbil is never still for very long. It is forever on the move, probing every nook and cranny of the cage, climbing the wire or digging in the dust.

TAKING THE GERBIL HOME

Regardless of the source from which the gerbil is acquired, common sense should prevail; on no account accept a gerbil just because it is being offered very cheaply. Be wary—there is probably some hidden reason why the gerbil is being offered at so low a price. There are of course genuine bargains, but these are very few and far between!

If arrangements have been made for you to collect a gerbil on your first visit to the seller, take along a suitable container in which to transport the gerbil home. Ensure that the carton or cage is easy of access and that the gerbil can be put into it without any trouble. There is nothing worse than trying to get a frightened gerbil into an opening that does not allow it to pass

Gerbils are naturally active and alert rodents. Beware of any that sits quietly in a corner, so unlike the frisky one shown here. Photo by D.G. Robinson, Jr.

easily. Wood is best, but if the container is a cardboard one, make sure that the edges and the corners are strengthened. Gerbils have an uncanny way of finding the weak spots in anything as vulnerable as cardboard and promptly show it by chewing their way out.

If you are buying more than one gerbil, be sure that they are both quite young or, if adult, that they are chosen from the same cage. Strange gerbils will fight as soon as they see each other, and you obviously want to prevent this. It does not make any difference whether a male and female, two females or two males are chosen. As long as they are acquainted with each other from the start, there should be no fighting. If there is no intention of breeding, then the two latter combinations are best.

If your journey home is to be a long one, provide some kind of bedding. Shredded tissue paper is perhaps the best material. A handful of food is very welcome, as is fresh water; in the absence of water, put in a piece of root vegetable. Ventilation is of paramount importance; if it is not adequate, your new gerbil could easily suffocate, but if it is too drafty, the gerbil could catch a cold or chill. Ventilation holes should be punched in the sides of the box at the top and bottom, providing for a steady flow of fresh air. If a metal box is used, make sure that any sharp edges are filed off flat or taped over, since serious injury can result if this is neglected. Do not be tempted to peep into the box on your way home! The gerbil will be quite all right as long as the box is held in an upright position and is kept steady. Any intrusion will only cause the gerbil more anxiety, since it will be frightened anyway.

INTRODUCING THE GERBIL TO ITS NEW HOME

Upon arriving home, give the gerbil some time to settle down. Leave it in its traveling box to recuperate from the journey. Put it somewhere warm and quiet

Although gerbils are far from being vicious, it will be best to handle them carefully at the beginning. They do bite when alarmed or frightened. Photo by D.G. Robinson, Jr.

and let it stay there at least half an hour. To introduce the gerbil to its cage is a straightforward procedure; however, if you are not sure that you can handle the gerbil correctly without any accidents, it may be easier to put the box inside the cage and let the gerbil find its own way out. When removing the gerbil from the traveling box, put it on a table so that if an accident should occur, there is no danger of the gerbil's falling or hurting itself. Take hold of the gerbil by the base of the tail and place it in the prepared cage. If the opening is restricted in size, it is much safer to remove the whole of the cage front. Leave the gerbil alone again for a while so that it can get accustomed to its new surroundings.

On the evening of the first day, feed the gerbil by merely filling up its food pot. Do not make any unnecessary sudden movement or noise, as this will make the process of taming harder. For the first week, continue feeding in this way, allowing the gerbil to come right up to your hand. Don't be tempted to stroke it at this stage! This should be tried only after the gerbil has more confidence. The second week should be spent in trying to get the gerbil to take food from your fingers. There is no short cut to this method of training, and great patience is required in order to receive the gerbil's complete trust. Most gerbils are great lovers of sunflower seed, and you should offer some. So instead of filling the food pot, remove it often and offer the gerbil sunflower seed from your fingers—say twice a day. At first, it will take the seed and run away to a corner of the cage to eat it. Keep repeating this practice, however, until the gerbil looks forward to the approach of your hand. When this is apparent, the food can be placed in the palm of the hand and the gerbil will stand on your hand and be perfectly at ease while feeding in this way.

There is a right and a wrong way to pick up a gerbil. And this is very important. The *right* way is to grasp hold of the tail near the base and swing the gerbil onto your hand or arm so that it crouches quietly on all four legs. **Never** let it dangle while you hold its tail. Being allowed to dangle not only frightens the gerbil but also causes it discomfort. The *wrong* way to pick up a gerbil is to grasp it by the tip of the tail. **Don't, don't** do this. A gerbil's tail is loosely covered with skin that peels away if pulled too hard. This is very serious and painful for the gerbil, and if it should happen, the kindest course of action is to have the animal painlessly destroyed. Sometimes extremely tame gerbils can be picked up by closing the hand around the body, but this method is not recommended for picking up gerbils that are strange to the handler, as they will bite in their efforts to get free.

A struggling gerbil can be injured if one unknowingly squeezes it tightly. This can result in fractures, dislocations and bruises. Photo by Dr. H.R. Axelrod.

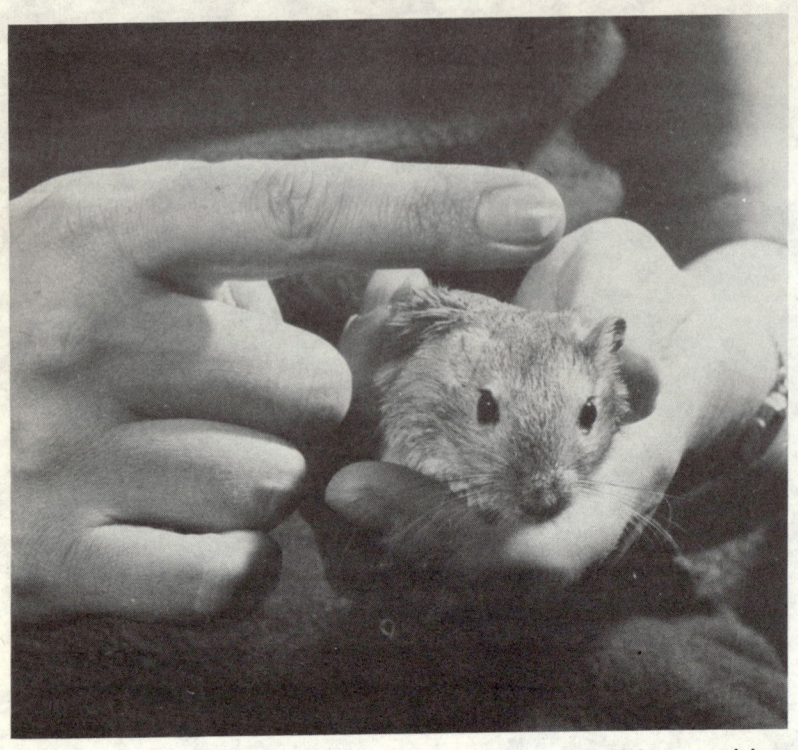

The process of taming gerbils can be hastened and improved by stroking the animal gently on its back. Stroking appears to have a calming or quieting effect on many small mammals.

Never hold a gerbil up to the face of a person—some people cannot stand the sight of rodents. Serious accidents can be caused by foolish pranks such as this. If you want to assure somebody that gerbils are perfectly harmless, do so by handling the gerbil in the normal way and show them that there is nothing to be afraid of. Young children love to cuddle all kinds of animals—but they can kill their pets with kindness by gripping them too tightly. Therefore, see that any such child is properly supervised during the handling period. Always handle gerbils over a table so that there is less danger of an injurious or possibly fatal fall.

A spotted mutation is known in gerbils, but a banded type (like this banded cinnamon hamster shown here) is yet to be produced. Photo by R. Hanson.

Accommodations

Gerbils are very adaptable and will live in almost any type of cage. There is a vast variety of cages to choose from, ranging from an old dish pan to the most expensive modern cage that ingenuity can devise for those with a large budget. The cage has a great effect upon the life of the gerbil in captivity; it should be roomy, light, escape-proof and, above all, easily accessible for cleaning. Of all the tasks connected with keeping gerbils, cleaning is the one that takes the most time. It can be a pleasure or it can be a bore, depending largely on whether the job can be done with ease and in a matter of minutes or whether it is difficult and takes quite a while—and of course it also depends on the mood with which you start it!

At feeding time the same applies—nothing is more laborious than having to take the cage apart in pieces just to replenish the food bowl. For the person who has only one or two pet gerbils, the cost of the cage is not usually important. The amateur breeder, on the other hand, cannot afford to lay out large sums of money on dozens of cages to house his innumerable gerbils.

CAGE SPACE

Gerbils will not breed satisfactorily if there is not enough space to accommodate the forthcoming young. For this reason a maximum of one gerbil to every thirty-six square inches of cage space must be the general rule. Pet gerbils are easily accommodated within this area, but the breeder may be presented with problems in this direction because he will not always have the available cage space.

TYPES OF CAGES

The types of cages one generally finds for sale in pet stores are usually advertised as suitable for hamsters or mice. This is the kind that should be looked for, as they are also suitable for gerbils. The material used in the construction of a cage is a point needing careful consideration. Today plastics are used perhaps more than any other material; they have many good points, but also one or two bad ones. Foremost, plastic is light in weight, easily washed during cleaning and holds heat to a certain extent. The main disadvantage is that the edges are easily gnawed if they are not protected.

The next most used cage is metal, which has the advantage of being chew-proof. But it is not a warm substance and, once the paint has peeled away, rust soon sets in. This is particularly true in those corners of the cage where the gerbil makes its toilet. A gerbil's urine is very concentrated and also acid; any bare metal subject to a contant deposit of urine is at the mercy of rust, and damage will soon appear. The metal cage can always be painted, but care must be taken to use a nontoxic paint. Some metal cages can be quite heavy, which is a disadvantage if the cage has to be moved often.

Lastly comes the wooden cage, which is particularly vulnerable to gnawing. This can often be prevented or reduced by covering the exposed edges with thin strips of metal. Wood is warm but can be absorbent, which is a disadvantage if cleaning out is delayed for any length of time.

Most modern cages can be taken apart for ease of cleaning. They are available in all sorts of designs, and the choice is merely a matter of preference. There are

Although wild guinea pigs very similar to these agouti guinea pigs still exist in South America, they have been domesticated for centuries, so many different varieties have been bred.

Examples of Abyssinian guinea pigs. The coat is very rough and some hairs extend from a central point resulting in the formation of whorls or rosettes in several areas of the body.

Another variety of guinea pig has a single rosette or whorl on the head; it is recognized as a crested guinea pig. Photo by Ray Hanson.

the simplest types, with plain wire fronts that slide in and out. There is also the "penthouse" type, which has two stories connected by a ladder—the idea here is that food and water are placed in the lower half and the gerbil sleeps in the top half. This, however, seldom works in the way it was intended, since the gerbil usually makes its bed on the lower half. New designs are produced often, and cages exist that have areas connected with a series of tunnels. As the gerbil population grows, new pieces can be added so that a large complex of apartments connected by tunnels is the end result.

Perhaps the most common cage is the ordinary aquarium. One of its great assets is its all-round visibility. But placed near a window in the sun, it can easily be turned into an oven . . . the effect of the sun's rays is increased both by the glass of the window and the sides of the aquarium. Although gerbils are great jumpers, they can rarely leap high enough to escape from a good sized aquarium. It is a wise precaution, however, to provide some sort of cover. Aquarium hoods can be bought from any tropical fish store. There are many advantages in buying such a hood, which is usually made of metal (and light metal at that) with an attached light socket and holes drilled for the correct flow of fresh air. Although modern all-glass aquariums are relatively light, they are still rather difficult to clean out properly, so for this reason fresh air is of great importance. The sawdust or whatever floor dressing is used should be kept reasonably fresh and clean for as long as possible. Without air the sides of the aquarium will steam up and obscure the view of the inmates; as the steam condenses, the water will run down onto the floor of the aquarium. Although sawdust will absorb some moisture, it will soon begin to smell, and cleaning out will therefore have to be done that much more often. The easiest way of covering the top of an aquarium, and a very practical

Gerbils will not hesitate to leave their cage when the opportunity exists—a good reason why a good cover is indispensable. Photo by D.G. Robinson, Jr.

The water vole is a cricetid rodent that lives along the banks of streams. Water voles are short-sighted but very good swimmers.

A water vole swimming toward its underwater burrow opening. Not all species of water voles build burrows with entrances below the water level.

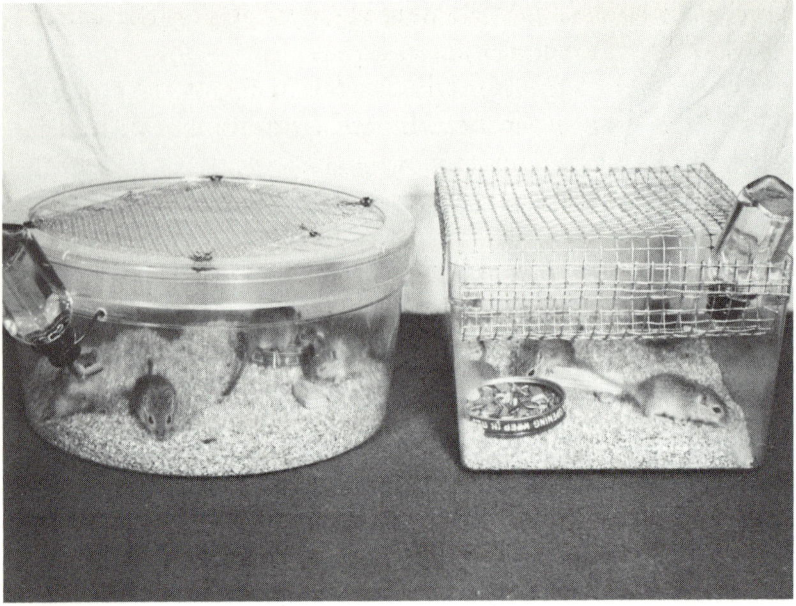

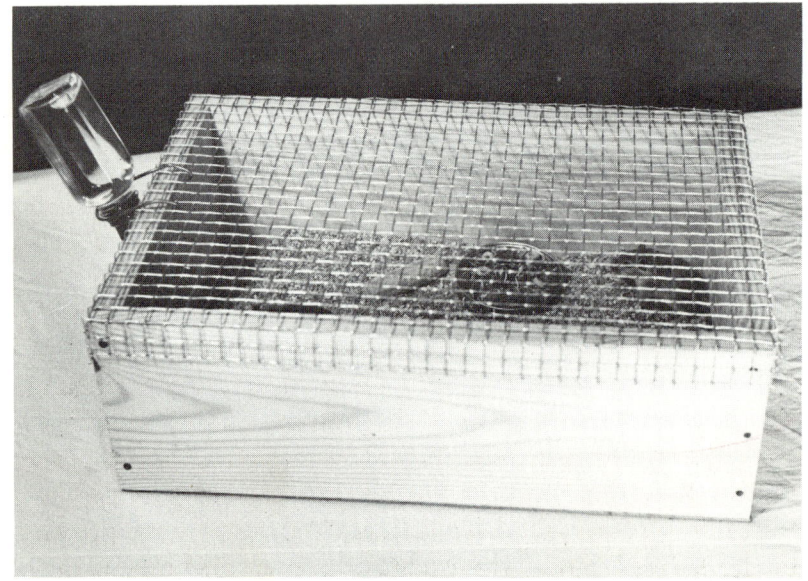

A sampling of cages which are sufficient for keeping a few gerbils in the home. A sturdy wooden box can be converted into a gerbil cage upon the installation of a secure cover and a spouted water bottle on one of the sides (bottom photo). Photos by D.G. Robinson, Jr.

one, is to enclose it with wire mesh which allows a free flow of fresh air and admits light.

If none of these methods of housing is selected, a very simple cage can be adapted from an old dishpan. The top is merely covered with wire mesh, as with the aquarium, and the edges are bent over around the side. This type of cage is, in fact, similar to those used in animal research stations and laboratories and has a lot to recommend it since it is light, easy to clean, and can moreover be stacked easily—one on top of the other in a breeding unit.

If the gerbil fancier is handy with woodworking tools, simple cages can be constructed very cheaply. Old drawers provide a ready-made unit. All that is to be done is for the front to be hinged or held in place with buttons made from pieces of wood. The top of the cage is again covered with wire mesh as before.

Cages can be stacked one on top of the other, but it is preferable to insert strips of wood between the cages so that fresh air can circulate. The ideal solution is to construct a permanent cage rack if you have the space for it. The framework of the rack should be constructed of two-by-two-inch lumber and the shelves supporting the cages made from one-inch lumber or boards. The size of the rack will depend upon the number of cages it has to accommodate and the amount of space available.

Another type of cage unit can be made which does not involve the use of a rack; this is the type used by bird breeders. The cages are made in block form and have removable fronts. These cages are made in a block of perhaps six, three along the top and three more underneath. The wire fronts can be bought in one piece as they are made for bird breeding cages and come in various sizes depending upon the size and species of bird that they are intended for. The wire front is easily fixed to the entire front of the cage with nails, allowing light

Another member of *Gerbillus,* dwarf or pygmy gerbil, is seen looking out of its natural burrow. Its burrow may be covered loosely with sand and can be difficult to locate.

Note the wild or natural fur coloration and pattern of this Egyptian gerbil *(Gerbillus)*. Desert-living mammals usually have white-furred abdomens, an adaptation to its habitat. Photo by R. Hanson.

← A nest of the greater Egyptian gerbil *(Gerbillus)* with babies that are fully furred but with closed eyes, and one of the parents, most probably the female.

A cage adequate for keeping and breeding gerbils. However, a bare wire mesh floor is not desirable; an appropriate floor which can hold the bedding should be installed. Photo by Dr. H.R. Axelrod.

to enter the full interior of the structure. A group of such cages has much to recommend it as being a great space and labor saver. Such cages do not have to be taken down during cleaning. All that needs to be done is for the front to be removed and the soiled contents swept into the garbage can. The cage can be constructed in one long length and then divided into sections with removable partitions. The advantage is that the entire length of the unit can be used to house a whole community of gerbils. For specialized breeding, the cages can be divided into sections so that mixing of the gerbils does not occur.

PAINTING

For the inside decoration of the cages, emulsion paint is the best material to use; it is non-toxic, dries fairly quickly and can always be repainted when dirty. The outside of the cages can also be painted in this way, but it is better to protect it fully with an oil-based paint.

Care must be taken that such paints do not contain lead, which is toxic. Suitable paints can usually be found in most paint stores—they are often sold for painting children's toys and furniture.

SIZE OF CAGE

Floor space is also a thing that should be taken into consideration when building cages for breeding gerbils. For a single pair the space given for the drawer-type

All-glass aquariums are excellent as gerbil quarters. Besides being draft-free from the sides, they can easily be equipped with covers that provide security—and they're easy to clean and disinfect.

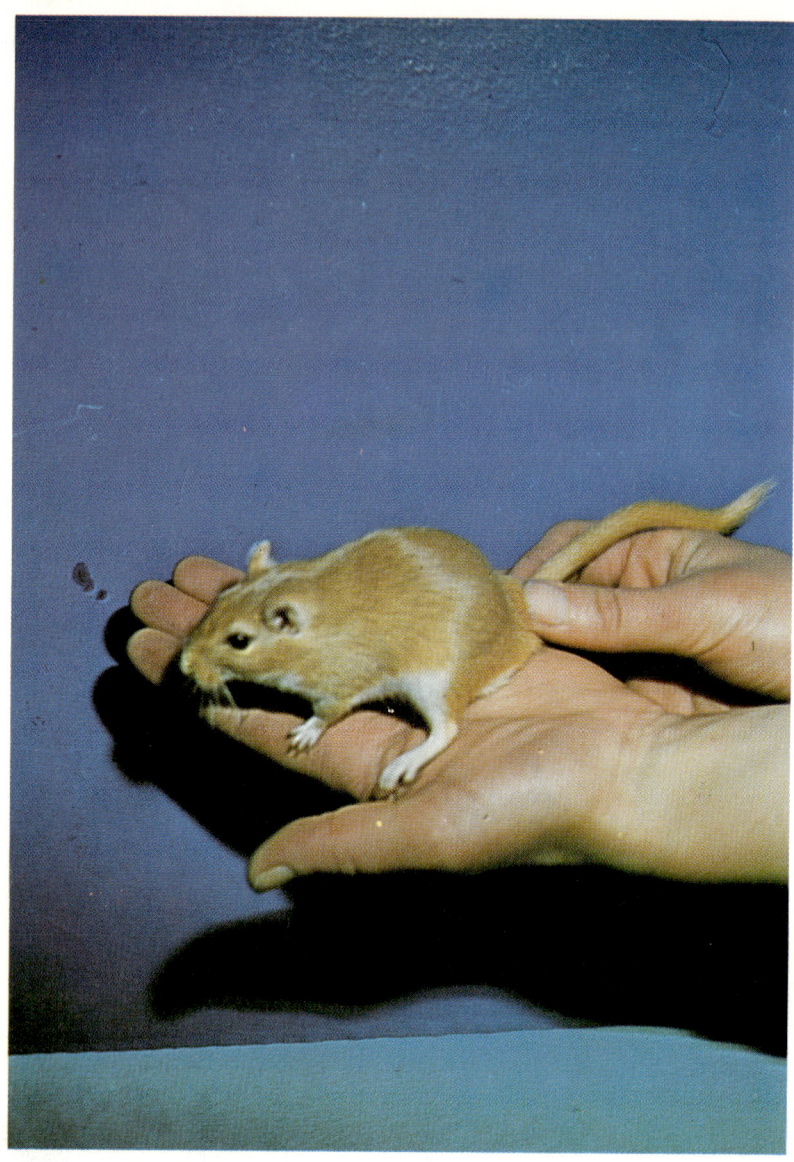

A coat that is sleek and glossy indicates good health. This gerbil is held correctly at the base of the tail, but being so active it has turned toward one side. Photo by R. Hanson.

Never buy a gerbil whose fur appears ragged and who lacks an alert disposition. Photo by R. Hanson.

cage is about the minimum—fifteen by ten inches, giving an area of one hundred and fifty square inches. The pair of gerbils will breed quite happily within this space. The resulting young must, however, be removed as soon as they are old enough to fend for themselves since if they are left with the parents overcrowding will stop the arrival of any more. Gerbils are very fussy about the amount of space they have allotted when kept in captivity. As soon as their numbers reach the maximum level, they will cease to breed. The smaller type of cage is, therefore, unsuitable for the serious breeder who wishes to breed his gerbil stock in a long continuous cycle. The unit cage is much more suited to this purpose as the number of animals can be allowed to reach quite a substantial level before any effect is felt by the breeding pair. Of course, the numbers of gerbils will not be allowed to reach such a high theoretical level as individuals will be removed periodically.

FLOOR DRESSING

Floor dressing is a matter of preference. Sawdust is the universal material and is accepted as the most practical of all floor dressings. It is absorbent, clean and, above all, pleasant to handle when dry and fresh. Once damp it gives off a smell rather like ammonia—but it should never be allowed to reach such a state.

There are three main types of sawdust: pine, coarse softwood and fine softwood. Pine sawdust is highly aromatic and reddish in color; it has the disadvantage that it is usually very fine in texture, so much so that it can sometimes cause irritation to the eyes and nose of gerbils if they kick it about. Coarse softwood sawdust is superior to any other; it is much warmer and softer and can absorb quite an amount of water before it becomes putrid. Being thicker in texture, it does not scatter as easily. Fine softwood sawdust is not as good and should

A gerbil digging into a coarse sawdust flooring, one type of desirable bedding material. Photo by D.G. Robinson, Jr.

be used only as a substitute.

Gerbils, as we have said earlier, are very clean in their habits and can be left for quite a while before cleaning becomes necessary. At a minimum, all that is required is the removal of the soiled areas. The entire contents of the cage must, however, be completely changed once it becomes impractical to remove the soiled areas.

There are other floor dressings that can be employed, but none of these is as practical as sawdust. The first one that springs to mind is sand; it is quite easily bought but is bulky and if damp can be heavy; it does not have the same absorbent quality as sawdust, but it does not smell when damp. When quite dry it can be a nuisance, however, as it

Gerbils are not large, and their claws are not dangerous. Gerbils won't bite, either, except perhaps under exceptional circumstances—such as to protect themselves. Photo by D.G. Robinson, Jr.

It is harmful to squeeze a gerbil this way; the more it wriggles, the greater will be the tendency to grip the gerbil tighter. Photo by R. Hanson.

Wood shavings are available at pet shops. They come in different size packages, are vermin free, very safe and convenient to use.

flies in all directions at the least movement. Gerbils housed in an aquarium can be safely provided with sand, as it cannot be thrown out and make a mess. Desert-like conditions can be simulated with sand and rock, and an attractive setting can be formed in this way. Sand, however, being cold to the touch, should only be used indoors where there is a constant source of heating.

Another floor dressing is peat, the fiber-like soil. It can be burned, but its more common use is as an additive to enrich garden soil. Its use in gerbil cages is becoming more and more popular. One of the drawbacks of peat is that it is not clean, and when very dry it gives off a very fine dust. The absorbent qualities of peat are high, however, and it has much to recommend it if the disadvantages can be overcome. White gerbils should never be housed in a cage with peat on the floor because it will stain their coats.

Wood shavings are another material often used on the cage floor. They have the same good points as sawdust and are quite easily obtained. Softwood chips are the best type to

A gerbil in the process of shredding a piece of woven material for the nest. Photo by G.P. Robinson, Jr.

Routine handling of gerbils reinforces the feeling of trust for their keepers. Photo by D.G. Robinson, Jr.

To hold a gerbil correctly, support its weight on one hand and with the other hand hold it at the base of the tail—never at the tip. Photo by R. Hanson.

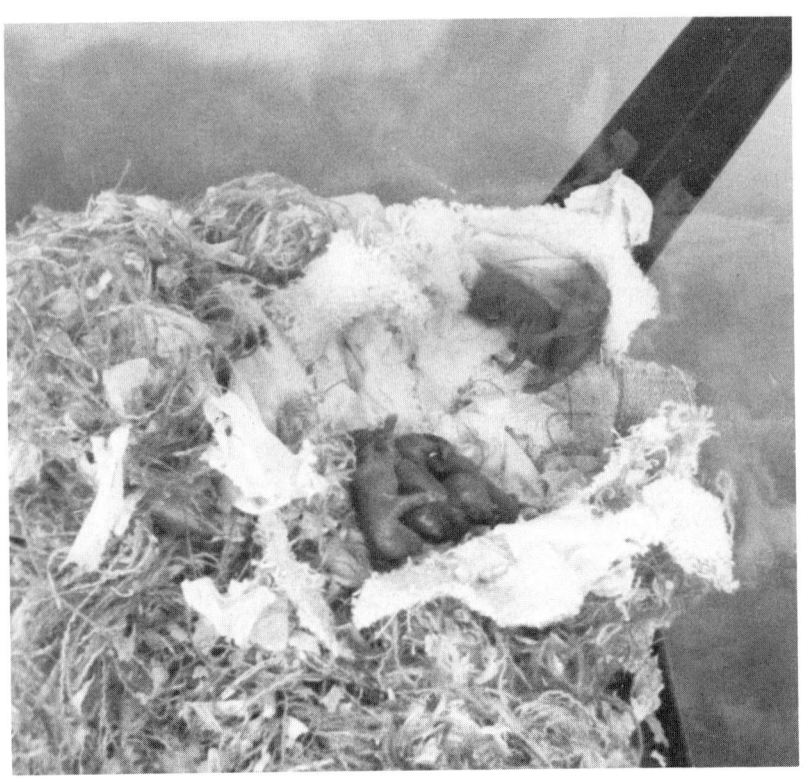

Appearance of a typical gerbil nest that has been pulled apart to expose the very young litter. Photo by D.G. Robinson, Jr.

use, being easier to handle and lying flatter on the floor. Cedar gives off a pleasant smell, although the chips are hard. Dry leaves have been tried, but they have little to offer; in time they crumble to dust and, because of the gerbil's habit of shredding anything soft, they do not last very long.

NESTING

If they are provided with enough suitable material, gerbils will build their own nest without the need to provide them with a nest box. However, some of the more nervous species which are hard to breed may benefit by the use of such a box. It should be easy to open for such necessary operations as inspection of the litter. The exact size will depend upon the size of the species for which it is intended; it should not take so much room as to leave little space for the gerbils to move easily around within the cage. Its entrance hole should be large enough to allow easy access; if it is too small, it will be difficult for the pregnant female to enter. If this is the case, there is the strong possibility that the litter will be born outside the nest box. The female may remove the newborn young to the safety of the nest box once she has become reduced in size—but she could just as easily kill them!

If no nest box is used, bedding should be provided in abundance. This is especially true for the Mongolian gerbil. Almost any soft material can be used for bedding purposes, although some are more durable than others. By far the best is burlap or sacking; it is warm, stays pretty dry and keeps its shape. There is no need to shred the burlap yourself; simply cut out a sizable piece and place it in the cage. The gerbils

Some type of nesting material is indispensable for gerbils being bred in "open-air" cages for the protection of the newborn from drafts. Photo by Dr. H.R. Axelrod.

When playing with an active gerbil it is necessary to have a firm grip on the base of the tail. If the animal were held by the tip of its tail, a sudden quick movement would strip the hairs from it or even damage the skin itself. Photo by R. Hanson.

The strong hind legs and foot are clearly shown, as is the length of the body, which is not always obvious when gerbils are in a sitting position. Photo by R. Hanson.

will have the time of their lives chewing it into pieces until there is nothing but a ball of fluff. Whenever the cage is cleaned out, a new handful of bedding should be provided; burlap soon becomes damp and subsequently sour.

Tissue paper is very popular as bedding, but if used in great amounts it can become quite an expensive commodity. Tissue paper does not keep its shape and soon gets scattered all over the cage floor.

Other types of paper can be used, but most of them are hard and offer little comfort. Almost any kind of cloth, however, can be offered to gerbils as bedding. They will shred it so it finishes up almost the same as burlap. Make sure, however, that it is colorfast and that dye will not run out of it. (This also applies to crepe paper that is colored. It will not only stain the gerbil's coat but may in instances cause poisoning.)

There are several materials that should never under any circumstances be used as bedding. Wool is one of these. It appears warm, soft and inviting, but if it is swallowed by a gerbil it will collect within the intestine and cause a severe blockage. Similarly, gerbils that are provided with cotton wool by inexprienced owners are liable to become constipated; if the blockage is not quickly removed, the unfortunate creature soon dies. Blockages of this kind are removed by administering of a mild laxative such as arrowroot or castor oil. It should be remembered that only a small amount of this should be given at a time, certainly more than once a day.

Wood wool (excelsior) is another dangerous substance. This is especially true when there are young gerbils in the nest; the edges can be very sharp indeed and can therefore cause serious injury to the young gerbil unprotected by a coat of fur. Wood wool is neither absorbent nor warm, so it is totally useless. Fiberglass matting should be provided under no circumstances; it is highly irritative to the skin.

Unless no longer needed, books should not be considered as toys for gerbils. They will surely chew the pages into shreds. Photo by Studio Morgan.

Whatever type of bedding is chosen, it must be changed regularly to ensure that all the cage stays in a healthy condition. It is no use putting clean floor dressing into a cage where the bedding is sour and smelly.

TOYS

Pet gerbils are the happiest when they are provided with toys and playthings to keep them occupied. Most pet stores sell toys that are intended for small birds, but they are also useful for pet gerbils. There are all kinds to choose from, including ladders, mirrors, balls and even

A type of commercially available cage that is suitable for gerbils.
Photo by R. Hanson.

little cars. Remember, though, that gerbils will gnaw these toys until they are completely demolished. If a mirror is provided, be sure to remove it before the edge of the glass is exposed or your gerbil may be injured by the sharp edges. Any sharp metal projections should be filed flat or removed completely. Simple inexpensive toys can be supplied by using any odd bits of scrap material; thread bobbins are very popular, as are cardboard boxes. The cardboard tubes from rolls of toilet

Samples of toys for small birds (budgies) which are perfect for gerbils too.

It is not too difficult to please gerbils. Anything can be amusing to these inquisitive creatures. Photo by Morgan Studio.

paper are also welcomed and find use as a tunnel. In fact, almost anything will be utilized as long as it is not dangerous.

Playwheels, however, are to be avoided like the plague. They are safe for mice or hamsters, but for gerbils they are a positive danger. Mice have semi-prehensile tails which can be kept out of harm's way. This is not so with gerbils. The tail is loose and easily gets caught up in the spokes of the wheel. In the animal's efforts to get free the tail gets more tightly trapped, with the sad and ugly result that it is often amputated. Let common sense be your guide in all matters of housing and toys and you will not go wrong.

An empty tin can, provided it has no sharp edges, is a practical gerbil toy. However, the type of exercise wheel shown is definitely not recommended and should be removed. Photo by D.G. Robinson, Jr.

Feeding Techniques

Nothing could be simpler than feeding gerbils; but it is also true to say that feeding can be as complicated as the owner wishes it to be. It all depends on what is sought by the type of feeding and what result the owner has in mind.

A breeder who has to feed several hundred gerbils will want to do it so that they are nourished and healthy enough to breed well, but because he has so many, he will have to keep the cost to a minimum. The person who keeps gerbils solely for exhibition purposes will not have such a large number, but they have to be kept in the pink of condition if they are to bring him credit on the show-bench. For the keeper of pet gerbils there are none of these problems. He can be much more choosy in the choice of food that he offers his gerbils.

Most species of gerbil do not store food, although there are some which have been known to practice this habit. Only very rarely will a gerbil over-indulge itself to such an extent that it makes itself ill.

Feeding times depend on the amount of spare time that the owner has for his charges. There is no hard and fast rule here, but generally once a day is sufficient. A good guide is to feed a tablespoon of food per gerbil per day. Gerbils have their own personalities: some will have a good feed upon being presented with a meal, others will take just a nibble here and there and never really eat great amounts in one sitting. They also have their own likes and dislikes. Some will eat all of one par-

Individual gerbils have their preferences for different types of food, so the best recourse is to provide them a little of everything so that no particular nutrient will be missing. Photo by Studio Morgan.

ticular food before any other, and the next gerbil will eat something quite different. This is not to say that the owner should pander to his animals' preferences. If he does, it could easily do more harm than good. Even we humans have our own favorite foods, but that does not mean that we can live on them for the rest of our lives. In correct feeding the aim is variety, plenty of variety. Gerbils that are fed the same type of food over and over again soon get out of condition, cease to breed in the normal manner and lose interest in life.

It is easy to fall into the trap of unimaginative feeding. The gerbils may look and behave quite normally, but on being given something new and different to eat, the result can be startling. If a colony of gerbils is kept in one cage, the first gerbil to find this new food will seize it and run into a corner to devour it greedily. Any other gerbil in the colony that happens to notice will then challenge the first gerbil for possession. In some cases a fight will ensue, often with serious results.

There is a vast variety of foods that can be offered to gerbils. The easiest way to feed them is to buy a pre-packaged mixture from your local pet store. The food itself is usually of a high quality, very clean and vitamin and mineral enriched. Such types of food are often sold for feeding hamsters or mice, but they are also quite suitable for gerbils. If a single gerbil or even a pair is kept, then it may be more convenient to buy in this way.

For the serious breeder there are two alternatives open. A number of pet food manufacturers mix their own feeds and sell them by weight in a plain bag or sack. These mixtures are cheaper than the packaged foods in small quantities and over a period of time prove more economical. A possible drawback of this type of food, usually called a laboratory diet, is that not all brands may be nutritionally complete. Be sure to read the labels carefully to compare ingredients used in different brands.

Another method involves buying in bulk to a certain extent and could appear at the outset to be costly. In fact, it works out very much cheaper in the long run. Storage space is required and must be dry, clean and vermin-proof. The food is bought in quantity and should consist of various types of grain. In this way a perfectly balanced diet can be maintained, specially formulated to provide the essentials for a healthy gerbil colony. Not only this, but the diet can be altered to suit any particular need. For instance, if it were felt that the stock was not breeding properly, this could easily be due to the fact that the diet contains too much fat. In such a

A typical food mixture for hamsters that is also appropriate for gerbils and other small mammals like rats, mice, etc. It includes sunflower seeds, wheat, oats, corn and some broken up dog biscuit. Photo by M.F. Roberts.

case the amount of offending foods can be slowly diminished until a happy medium is reached. The main problem is food storage. It would be nonsensical to buy a large quantity of food only to let it go bad because the storage is damp. Disease-carrying vermin can transmit many types of disease through being allowed to eat the stored food. By far the best method is to put the food into metal containers. These should have a tight-fitting lid with tiny holes punched in the top for ventilation.

Mixing your own food is a matter of common sense. Start with the basic items and add to them the desired quantity of whatever is required. For feeding gerbils the basic foods are oats, rabbit pellets and crushed corn. Oats are available in two forms. There are clipped oats, which are in fact the whole grain merely opened slightly. There are also crushed oats, which are the better of the two. Crushed oats are self-explanatory—the whole oat grain is crushed until the husk is removed. The grains should not, however, be crushed so flat as to disintegrate upon contact with the hands, nor should they be so lightly crushed that the husk is left intact. Waste is a problem that unfortunately cannot be avoided as the husks are sometimes included in the weight. This can be irritating when crushed oats are bought because one sometimes has to pay for the useless part as well.

Oats are rich in carbohydrates, which promote heat and energy within the gerbil's body. Care, however, must be taken not to give too much carbohydrates because any excess is stored within the body as extra fat. It is this fat which causes difficulty in breeding; many females have trouble giving birth to their young because they are too fat internally. Carbohydrates are based on carbon, hydrogen and oxygen compounded as starch and sugar. These substances along with protein (amino acid, complex compound of hydrogen, carbon, nitrogen, oxygen and other elements) provide energy and repair tissues. Oats contain about 62% carbohydrates, 12% protein, 6% fat, 2% salt and 15% water. They constitute one of the basic feeding stuffs.

Another food mixed in with oats is wheat. This also is a food very rich in carbohydrates and made up of the following: 70% carbohydrates, 13% protein, 2% fat,

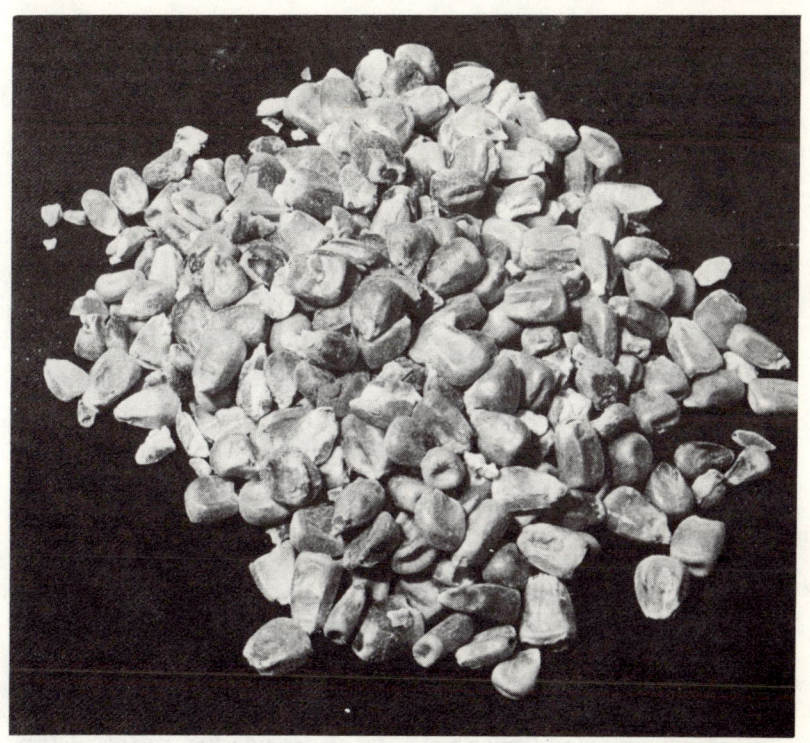

Although corn is a good source of carbohydrates and oil, giving it to gerbils in its natural grain form has been proved wasteful. Photo by M.F. Roberts.

1.7% salt and 14% water. Corn is usually available in two forms. First, there is the whole corn grain. If it is fed whole to gerbils, they have an undesirable habit of eating the heart and leaving the rest. This does them little real good and is also wasteful. A more satisfactory way of offering corn is to buy corn flakes. It has two main advantages: the first is that it is available in smaller quantities than whole-grain corn, which makes for cheaper buying and easier storage. The second advantage is that the entire grain is eaten and nothing is left to waste. Gerbils enjoy corn in flakes, and it should be included in the diet. The carbohydrate content of 65% makes it a very valuable basic foodstuff. It also contains 10% protein, 7% fat, 1.7% salt and 14% water.

When these three foods are mixed, they make the base for a balanced diet. Barley is sometimes substituted in place of any one of the three staples as it is also high in carbohydrates and other basic materials. Rabbit pellets are a manufactured food that is specially formulated to give all the benefits of the vitamins and minerals of natural foods with the additional benefit it is easily stored and simple to feed. The pellets are made from the waste that usually is thrown away, including the chaff from various milled grains. Chaff is boiled with grass meal and, as it cools, the essential vitamins and minerals are added. The mash is then mixed and fed through a machine which squeezes the material through a nozzle and then dices it into tiny pieces. When dry the pellets are quite hard and can be packaged for sale. Certain pellets contain antibiotics which are added to counteract coccidiosis, which is a protozoan disease that attacks most mammals. These pellets can be used in place of the basic feeding mixture or they can be added to it so that the nutritious balance is evened up.

We can now move on to the more specialized foods that contain carbohydrates and more of the other properties. Their addition has the effect of evening up the balance even more and so giving the diet a more stable feeding value. The proportions of these foods should be as follows: 10% sunflower seed, 10% corn flakes, 5% barley, 25% rabbit pellets, 25% wheat and 25% oats.

The first of these additives is sunflower seed. If a gerbil is given a preference in its food, it will go for the sunflower seed every time. This seed is often a large part of parrot food. There are two types of seed, stripped and plain. These are variations that only apply to the outer casing and have little effect on the quality of the seed inside. Sunflower seed is very rich in fat and carbohy-

Sunflower seeds are almost always present in commercial food mixes for small mammals and birds. Gerbils love to nibble on these seeds especially. Photo by D.G. Robinson, Jr.

Gerbils, show gerbils in particular, can be given a basic food mixture consisting of millet, oats, and other seeds, besides some sunflower seeds of course.

drates and should be fed with discretion. Its breakdown is as follows: fat 21.5%, carbohydrates 21.4%, protein 16%, salt 2.6%, water 14%. Sunflower seed is good for young growing gerbils and should also be fed to nursing females. The fats it contains have a higher percentage of carbon, which has the effect of doubling the energy value, so it is valuable in this respect.

Various other kinds of seeds can be fed to gerbils, but they should be regarded as a treat rather than a daily food. Some, such as linseed, tend to raise the body temperature if given in excess, but their valuable oil content provides excellent feeding properties for the hair and promotes fur growth, giving it a healthy sheen. Among the more common types of seeds there are parakeet or budgie seed (sometimes known as millet), plain canary seed, rape seed, hemp and teazle. Such small seeds are very useful if the gerbil keeper is also an exhibitor. These seeds will help to maintain his stock in the highest possible condition.

Fresh green food is a must for all gerbils. It contains various kinds of minerals that are essential for the proper bodily functioning of the gerbil. About thirteen are known to be minerals used by the body. These include zinc, copper, iron, calcium, potassium, iodine, sulphur, magnesium, chlorine, sodium and manganese. Some, such as calcium, promote bone growth, while others, of which chlorine is a good example, help break down food to be absorbed within the body.

Green food contains a great amount of water, sometimes as much as 86%. Experiments have been carried out to determine whether gerbils can exist solely on dry foods, like oats and wheat, together with plentiful supplies of green food. The results are very revealing in that gerbils fed on this diet alone can live quite happily. They do not, however, achieve the same growth rate, nor do they appear to be in such good condition as gerbils that are given water to drink.

There are endless types of green food, which are split into two main groups. The vegetables that we ourselves eat form the main group , and the wild plants that grow in fields and lawns are the other. Good vegetables for gerbils are lettuce, cabbage, carrots, turnips and beets. Whichever greenstuff is offered, it must be washed well to remove any insects or dirt that can lodge in the leaves and roots. It is of great importance that green food is dried properly; if it is not, it can give rise to severe diarrhea. Large amounts of cabbage can also provoke stomach upsets, so it is much better to feed it little and often than to feed a lot infrequently. Root crops such as carrot and turnip give the gerbil something nourishing on which it can also sharpen and clean its teeth.

Wild plants should be collected with great care. It is too easy to pick plants that grow by the wayside without fully realizing to what they have been exposed. Dogs and cats often foul them, and there is also the pollution from car exhausts and insecticides. Whenever possible, pick wild plants from a field. If you are not sure of the identity of such wild plants, leave them alone. It is better to leave your gerbils without green food than to risk poisoning them by giving them plants that contain harmful ingredients. The list of safe wild plants includes the following: chickweed, dandelion, dead nettles, groundsel, knapweed, shepherd's purse, clovers and grasses. As with vegetables, these wild plants should be washed and dried thoroughly. Many of them could have been treated with pesticides and fertilizers which could prove deadly if left on the leaves.

All the foods mentioned in this chapter contain vitamins in one form or another. Vitamins are naturally present in the foods but are also manufactured within the animal's body. The five main groups of vitamins have the well-known vitamins A, B, C, D and E. Vitamin A is present in fresh green food and in cod liver oil. Vitamin B (a group of several different vitamins) is also found in green food, most cereals and such grains as wheat, oats and barley. Vitamin C is made within the gerbil's body and is also extracted from green food, especially fruit. Vitamin D is again produced within the body, but it cannot be made there without the help of sunlight; cod liver oil is a rich source of this vitamin. Vitamin E is present in the grain of cereals and also in

Coltsfoot

Shepherds Purse

Yarrow

Dandelion.

Clover

Some edible green foods that gerbils can feed upon. Greens should always be washed before offering to any pet animal to ensure the removal of harmful insecticides or other contaminants.

Compressed pellet food may be nutritionally complete, but some gerbils may find them unappetizing after prolonged use. Gerbils seem to love a variety of foods instead. Photo by M.F. Roberts.

fresh green food; it is an aid to fertility and reproduction.

Provided that a balanced diet is fed to gerbils, there should never be a deficiency in any of the five vitamin groups. Some keepers advocate, however, the use of vitamin supplements as an addition to dry food. Certainly their use will prevent any deficiency within the diet. There are many forms of vitamin supplements on the market, many of them being based on brewer's yeast and packed in powder form. A feeding guide usually comes with these products; if the instructions are followed, there should be no problems.

Fish liver oils are rich in certain vitamins but require careful dosages. Halibut liver oil is made much more potent if a small quantity of wheat germ oil is mixed with it. Cod liver oil should be used with discretion; too much can in fact quite negate the benefits of the vitamins present in the normal foods. If cod liver oil is left in direct light it soon loses all its valuable properties and then becomes rancid.

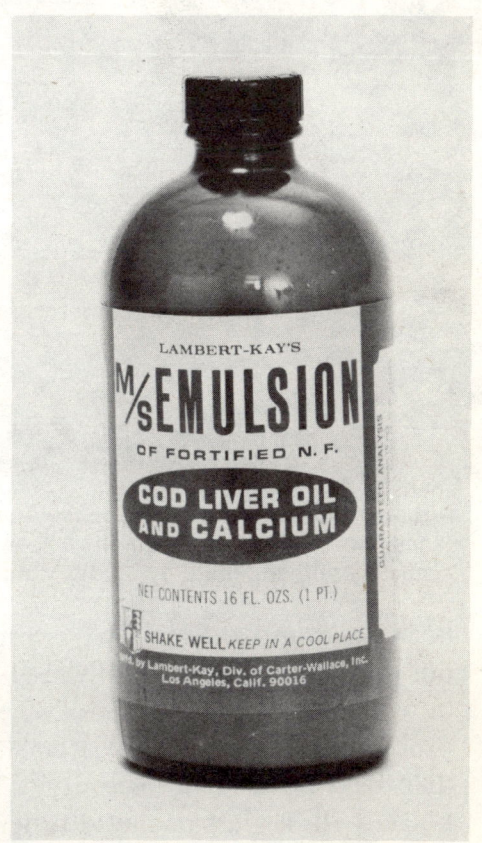

Gerbils, like other pets, occasionally require nutritional supplements like cod liver oil or vitamins even if they are maintained on a reasonably well-balanced diet.

Feeding vessels are a matter of personal preference; they are useful in some ways and a nuisance in others. Gerbils are improvident in that, when given water or food in a bowl, they will only drink or eat what they require and the rest gets covered with sawdust or whatever is on the cage floor. The floor dressing soon

Although the type of feeding vessel used is not of critical importance, it is best to provide gerbils a heavy feeding utensil that is not easily overturned. Photo by Studio Morgan.

becomes damp and smelly from spilt food or water, and not only that but the gerbils are without water until the bowl is cleaned and refilled—whereupon the same thing probably happens again! For situations like this, the drip-feed bottle is a necessity. This device is simply a bottle with a glass or metal tube inserted into the stopper, the action of surface tension of water in a small tube keeps the water from running out. The bottle is filled with water and the tube inserted in the bottle top where it is sealed with a rubber stopper inside the top. The whole bottle is then turned upside down, allowing the water to run to the end of the tube. This device is attached to the cage with the tube protruding into the in-

A gerbil drinking water from a drip type drinking bottle. If you wish to avoid frequent changes of bedding, never give gerbils water in shallow pans. Photo by D.G. Robinson, Jr.

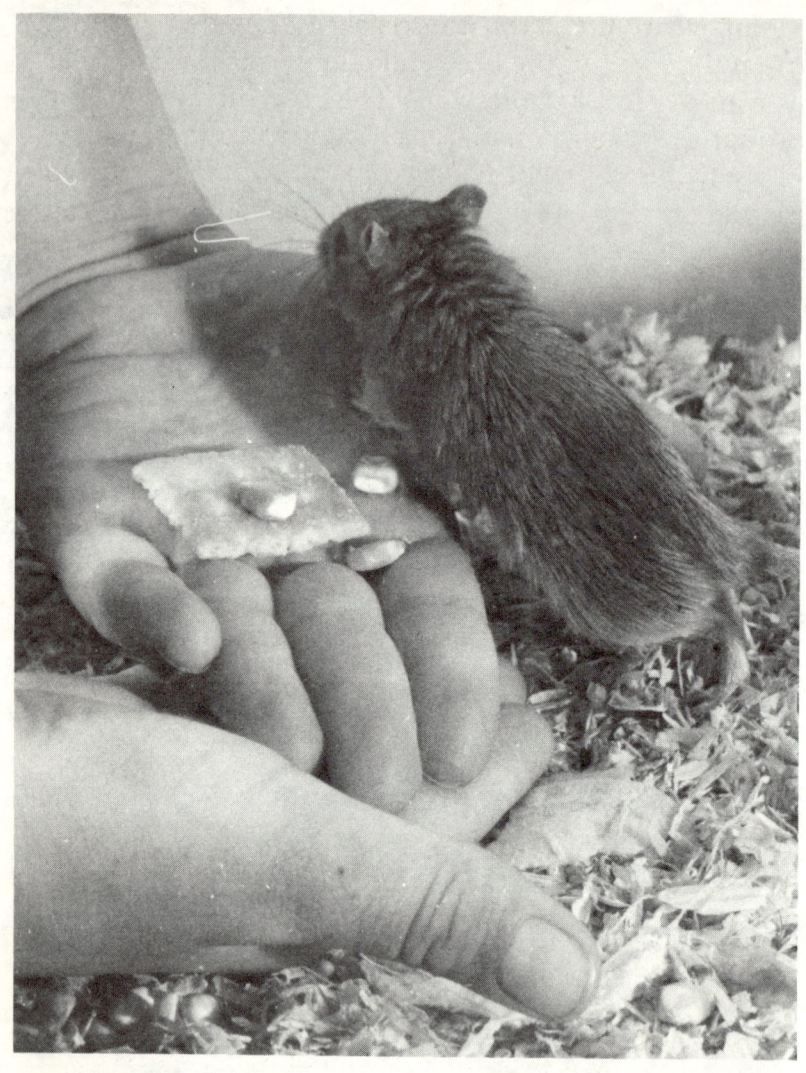

Occasional tidbits like crackers and other dry food are relished by gerbils. However, you should refrain from offering any type of sticky and very sweet food. Photo by D.G. Robinson, Jr.

terior where the gerbil can reach it. The gerbil drinks from the spout of the tube and only receives as much as it wants to drink at one time. The great advantage here is that the water remains clean and the cage stays dry. Only if through poor housekeeping sawdust is allowed to pile up near the mouth of the tube and cover it can the water be drawn out by capillary action and the cage once more becomes damp. Also, even hard rubber stoppers and plastic bottle caps are not immune to the gerbil's teeth, so the end of the bottle must be kept outside the cage.

Pet gerbils can be fed all sorts of tidbits, but these must be given to them with great discretion. Sweet things such as candy and chocolate are not good for gerbils no matter how much they may appear to like them. Table scraps are a completely different matter; there is no end to the choice that can be given. Meat, cheese, bread, etc., all contain nourishment; any kind of cooked meat can be fed with confidence, though it should be cut into fine pieces before being put into the usual mixture. Bread is better if it is left to go dry and then baked hard in the oven since it provides something on which the gerbils exercise their teeth. Wholewheat bread is best as it contains wheat germ. Cheese can either be grated or diced and fed as a tidbit. Mashes are an economical way of feeding gerbils (but not all will eat them), when all the scraps are mixed together to a thick pasty consistency. The mix is then dried off by adding a few handfuls of oats until firm to the touch. On no account should wet sloppy mashes be fed as they are a source of stomach upsets.

Feeding is really a matter of common sense. If the gerbil keeper is unsure of the suitability of a certain food, it is safer to leave it out altogether.

Breeding and Management

Breeding gerbils, or many other animals for that matter, is often taken much too casually. Raising a litter of young gerbils can be a most rewarding experience—or one that ends in heartache and sorrow. The pet gerbil keeper is advised to think carefully before allowing his animals to breed.

When the decision has been made to go ahead, the number of litters should be closely restricted. There are one or two sound reasons for this. The number of gerbils offered for sale has escalated to such an extent that it is very difficult to find homes for surplus stock. Many have been the times when an unsuspecting gerbil breeder has placed a cage full of youngsters on the pet store counter, only to be told that they are not wanted. In such situations, the gerbils must be painlessly destroyed, surely a waste of life. If the owner of the gerbils decides to try to keep them all, a serious situation will quickly arise. They will soon become a tax on time, money and food, with the result that the owner's interest goes, the gerbils become neglected and everybody loses all around. This state of affairs can easily be avoided without detracting from the great enjoyment that gerbil breeding gives.

Right from the start, common sense should prevail. If the idea is merely to keep two gerbils, it is much simpler to obtain a pair of the same sex. If introduced during infancy, they will not fight and will live together quite happily. If breeding on a limited scale is the objective, however, a pair of gerbils of either sex will occupy

The breeding of compatible pairs is of prime consideration to ensure the safety of parents to be. Photo by Studio Morgan.

the cage; it is wise to separate the male from the female a few days before a litter of young is expected. In this way a second mating will be prevented when the young are newly born, as is the normal practice with the Mongolian gerbil. If breeding is to be commenced at a later stage, it may be advantageous to keep a young male and female from the last litter. The original male can, of course, be reintroduced to his mate, but often this is impossible, as fighting breaks out. If she will not accept him in a strange cage, the female should be placed in the male's cage along with her estranged mate. If this fails, there is no alternative but to keep trying at regular intervals. The male should not be put into the female's cage. She will quickly resent his presence and attack him without provocation.

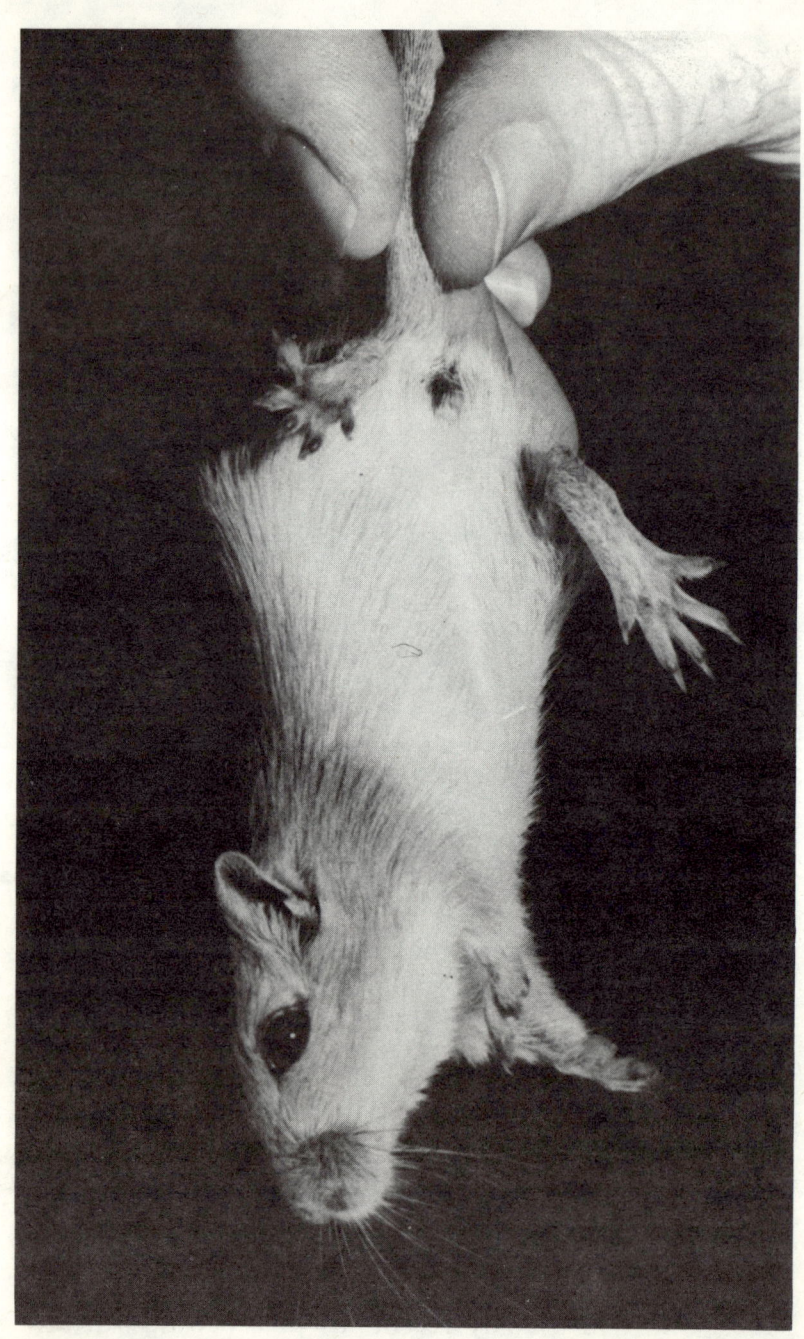

Ventral view of a female gerbil. Photo by D.G. Robinson, Jr.

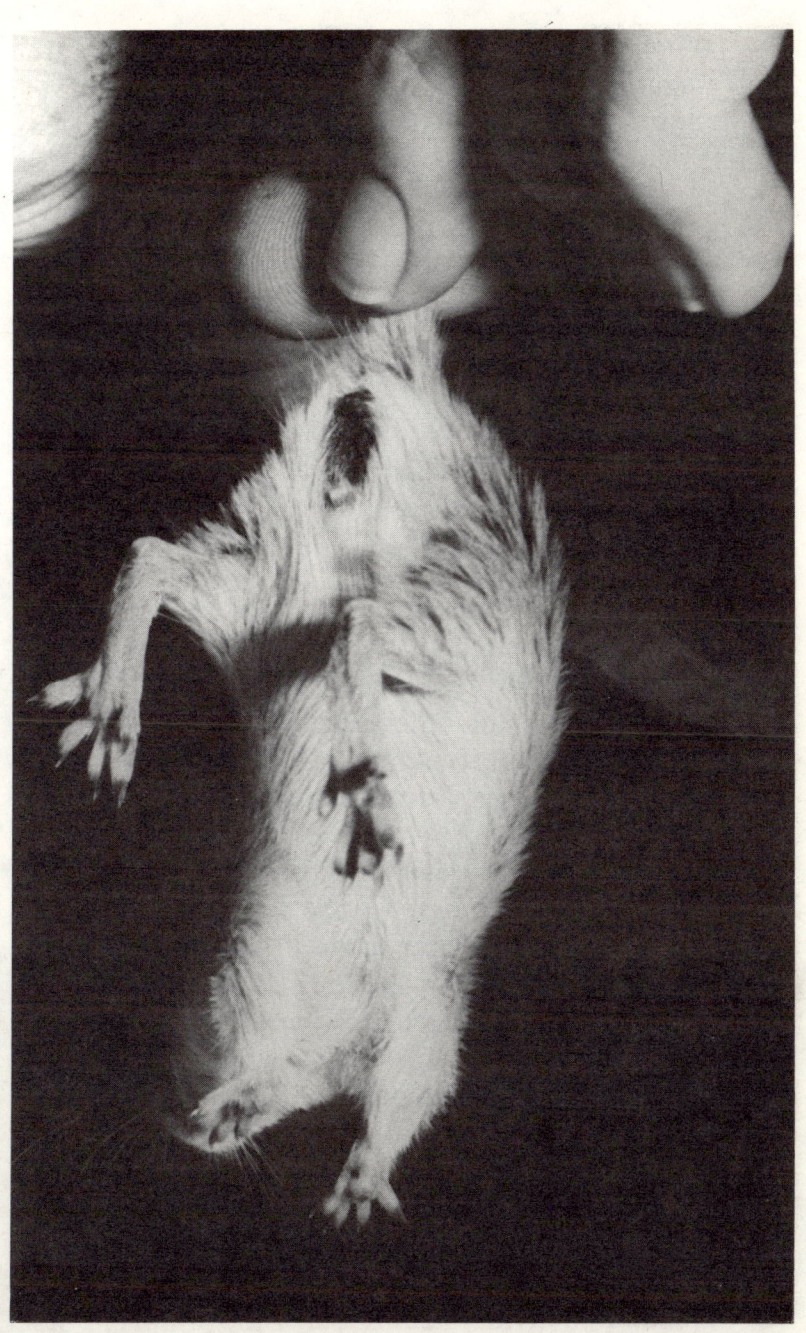

Ventral view of a male gerbil. Photo by D.G. Robinson, Jr.

When dealing with those species of gerbil that are not gregarious but lead solitary lives, the situation is made somewhat easier. The females can be introduced to the male at regular intervals and in this way the number of litters is controlled and the situation of having large numbers of surplus stock does not arise.

Breeding gerbils can be a trying business when the animals do not cooperate for one reason or another. One person can quickly become overstocked, as his gerbils will breed regularly. Another person, on the other hand, will not be able to tempt his gerbils to breed no matter what he does to encourage them. The reason for the erratic breeding periods in some captive gerbils is not fully understood. A number of factors may exist which, when combined, trigger the reproductive instincts. Mongolian gerbils are perhaps less susceptible to changes in environment than any other species. They have been known to breed when housed outside in the coldest weather; at the other extreme, they have been bred in temperatures exceeding 80 °F. In or out of doors, however, the problems seem to be the same and no sure way has been found to overcome them.

For the owner who wishes to breed only a limited number of gerbils, the best way to start is to obtain a pair of youngsters from the same litter. Adult gerbils unrelated to each other are very difficult to mate. Upon introduction, they will generally circle one another, sniffing the ventral areas. Usually one will try to achieve dominance by pushing the other onto its back. This is when trouble starts, for a fight often follows; left to their own devices, they could fight to the death. Gerbils can inflict quite horrific injuries upon each other in a very short period of time. Once in combat, they seem to lock together and only part to lick their wounds. Using the bare hand to divide them is asking for trouble in the form of bitten fingers—use a stick and/or gloves. As

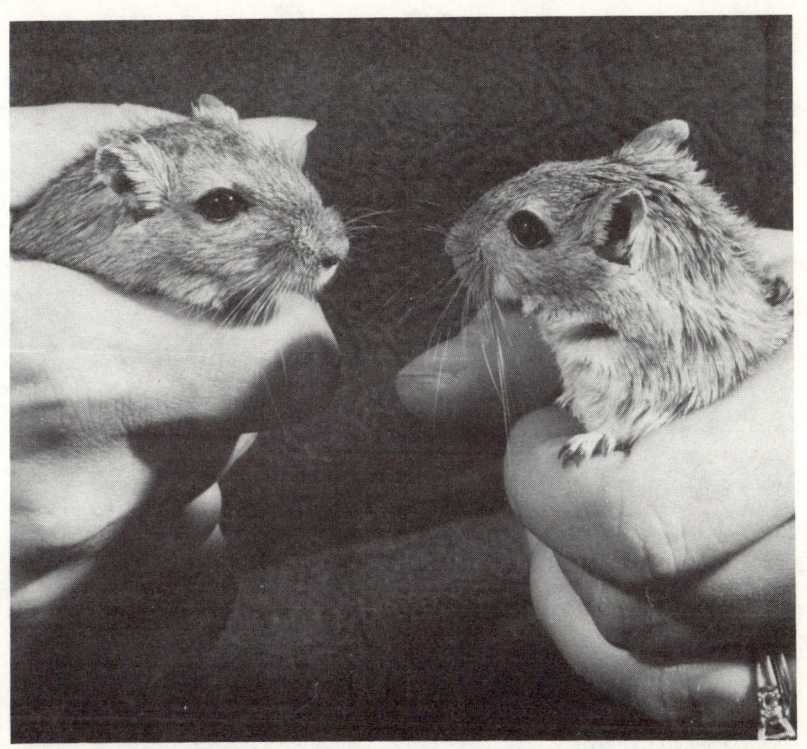

Sometimes it takes several attempts before a pair of gerbils will tolerate one another. The initial reaction can be observed by putting them face to face. Photo by D.G. Robinson, Jr.

soon as peace has been restored, the gerbils should be put back into their own quarters and not introduced again until they have settled down and forgotten their previous encounter. But fighting does not always occur on the first introduction, and the pair may settle down amicably without any trouble. Young pairs of gerbils that have grown up together will only fight very rarely once the adult stage is reached. The only course of action to take when animals fight is the patient and persistent introduction of the pair to each other until they finally accept each other's presence. The pair-bond in gerbils is extremely strong and lasts throughout the whole of its natural life span of three to four years.

A pair of gerbils in an isolated cage can take care of the litter without the threat of having other active gerbils endanger the young.

Colony housing has now become the accepted way of breeding gerbils. Colonies of gerbils will include as many as two or three pairs plus perhaps six immature individuals making up a colony of about twelve gerbils in all. At one time it was thought that the colony system aggravated jealousy between two females who sometimes bullied the male to death. This idea is a fallacy since two females and a male will in most cases live quite happily together. The obvious advantage in colony breeding is that much less space is required.

The disadvantage is that the precise parentage of any litters so reared in this way remains in doubt. Since female gerbils of a colony give birth in the same nest as other female members of the group, there are very often youngsters of all kinds of different ages in the nest at the same time. Also, breeding goes on fast, and if there are half-grown youngsters still in the nest when a new litter arrives the newborn sometimes get neglected and consequently kicked about the cage. There is also the danger, of the young being killed by any gerbil in an aggressive mood.

Colonies flourish easily as long as a cage of sufficient size is used. Space is very important; if it is too cramped, the gerbils will cease to breed once their numbers have reached a certain level. A thriving colony can be started from just a single pair. When the first litter has left the nest, they are allowed to stay with their parents until they themselves in turn breed. Thus quite a number of gerbils are reared in one large cage.

A colony of gerbils in one common accomodation. However, regular culling is needed to prevent overcrowding in a fixed area of space. Overcrowding inhibits reproduction and encourages fighting. Photo by Dr. H.R. Axelrod.

Gerbils are monogamous and, despite cramped quarters, they seem to enjoy each other's company most of the time. Photo by D.G. Robinson, Jr.

Young adult gerbils are sexually mature at between nine and twelve weeks of age. This is the time when the intended pairs should be introduced to each other. At this age, there is little danger of fighting and so much trouble is avoided. When a young pair that is sexually mature is left together, do not automatically expect them to breed from the onset. It may take up to six months before a litter is produced, and even then the results may be disappointing. Inexperienced gerbils, parents for the first time, sometimes neglect their litter of young. This does not usually happen with the second litter, which is reared with no trouble.

It is generally accepted that the act of mating takes place about five in the evening, but of course there are exceptions. The sex act itself is very brief but, because it is repeated time and time again, it can easily be observed. The period that the female gerbil is receptive to the male is rather obscure, but it is estimated that she comes

A mother gerbil nursing one of her pups. At this stage she needs nourishing food and plenty of green food. Photo by M.E. Ostrow.

into heat once every four to ten days. There is no hard and fast rule regarding the length of the gestation period when the female carries the unborn young. It varies between 24 and 26 days in general but may be even shorter in the smaller species. By the time the litter of young is due to be born, the female will have almost doubled her normal weight of three or four ounces. Her sides will look as though they are about to burst. Young gerbils usually arrive during the night or early morning, but many litters also come into the world during the day. The male of the pair will keep a respectful distance from the nest while the birth is actually taking place. During this time the female will be fully occupied and will soon have a nest full of wriggling hungry babies.

The infant gerbils do not have any teeth when they are born but rely entirely upon the supply of mother's milk. The babies are both blind and deaf at this early stage but make up for this with a lot of noise, mostly high-pitched squeaks. Newborn gerbils only measure about half an inch, but their rate of growth is quick. Within a matter of days the skin darkens as the fur grows. At about five to six days the whole of the body will have a coat of very light brown fur, and the body will measure about one inch. The limbs and tail are still short and remain like this until the young are mature (three months of age).

Young gerbils are tough little creatures and need to

Any type of material that can possibly soil the fur of white gerbils especially should not be used. Photo by Studio Morgan.

A typical container suitable for keeping gerbils. The wire mesh on top prevents gerbils from jumping out and also provides exercise when they swing from it, holding on with their teeth. Photo by R. Hanson.

Gerbils seldom neglect their young. Shown is a mother gerbil washing its baby. Photo by D.G. Robinson, Jr.

A normal position of a gerbil sitting on its litter, a means of providing warmth and protection. Photo by D.G. Robinson, Jr.

be since they take a lot of bumping about from the mother, who is quite prone to upset the nest and kick the babies in the process. If the young are without fur and are left stranded outside the nest, there is a danger that they will catch cold. The female will, however, usually cover up the nest and replace the youngsters; if she does not, you can safely put the young back yourself. Mongolian gerbils are very cooperative in this respect and accept handling of the young from a few days old. But the lesser-known species are much more worried by human interference and may resent it so much that they will kill and eat the whole litter.

The behavior of swinging overhead is not peculiar to gerbils (above, photo by Hanson); hamsters (below) behave likewise.

Gerbils enjoy toys. A red plastic tunnel provides endless fun to this male and female living together in complete harmony. One plays as the other feeds. Photo by R. Hanson.

From the moment the litter of young gerbils is born, the female's rations should be increased accordingly. At first only a small increase will be enough, but as the babies start to grow their demands on the female will increase daily. By the time they are five days old the demand will have almost reached its peak. At about ten days old their eyes will start to open and their ears will begin to stand up on their heads. They will be able to hear perfectly but will not be able to see well.

Play is an important part of a young gerbil's life, and young gerbils never seem to tire of fighting each other; no matter how often they are nipped by their brothers and sisters, they will always go back for

Close-up of immature gerbils of different ages; a naked newly born example and an older, already furred individual. Photo by D.G. Robinson, Jr.

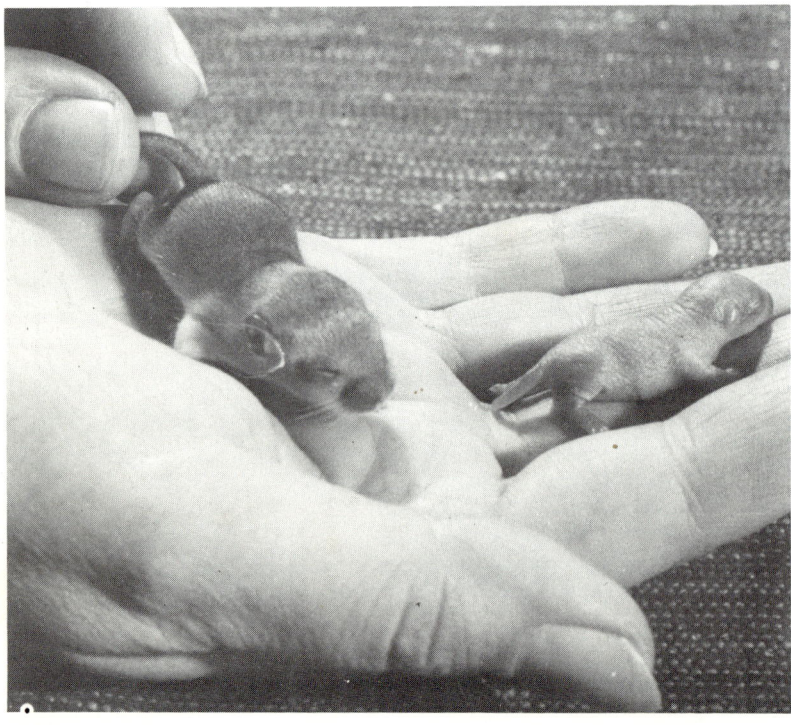

Although their eyes are still closed, baby gerbils are already active and may crawl away from the mother.

Openings are always attractive to gerbils. Any opening should be smooth-edged and large enough to exclude accidental strangulation.

A quick leap and the gerbil is hanging from the wire and gnawing away with its sharp teeth. This proves the need for a strong and reasonably heavy cover. Photo by R. Hanson.

A golden gerbil at play on a plastic container. Photo by R. Hanson.

Young gerbils spend much time playing with each other and with their parents; the male parent indulges less actively in this activity. Above and opposite page photos by D.G. Robinson, Jr.

another tussle. The father gerbil, left with female and babies, is treated more or less as an object of fun to play with. He is remarkably tolerant in this respect and will just sit there while his young family pulls him this way and that. The male does not take an active part in the rearing of a litter, but he will act as nursemaid should the need arise.

At around two weeks of age the young gerbils will begin to eat solid food for the first time. Careful watch

Gerbils use their forepaws to eat. This one is deftly removing the kernels of sunflower seeds from the husks, as can be seen from the scattered debris. Photo by R. Hanson.

Frontal view of a gerbil standing beside a stuffed toy. This type of toy is not safe from being torn apart by a gerbil. A woolly or cottony stuffing when ingested could cause intestinal blockage. Photo by D.G. Robinson, Jr.

It will be easier for gerbils to gnaw on slices of fruit, for example apple, rather than a whole fruit which is too large and very slippery. Photo by Studio Morgan.

should be kept on them at this stage to ensure that they are all feeding properly. The female's milk will have dried up by now, and if one or two of her litter have not learned to eat solid food they will suffer. (Fresh water should always be available to a family of gerbils; they will drink a surprising amount, and it is vital for continued health.)

Complete weaning should take place around the 28th day, so do not be tempted to remove the young any earlier than this. The young gerbils can be housed in the same cage if they are not to be separated from their parents. But the arrival of another litter may present problems with space and, therefore, the last litter should be taken away as soon as the 28th day is reached.

To ensure that the young gerbils are kept healthy, their food should be slightly enriched. Additives that can be put into the normal diet can include canary seed, bread that has been soaked in milk, biscuit crumbs and

A simple nesting box used for breeding small birds can be used by nervous gerbils.

cause of cannibalism; the immature parent is quite at a loss when she suddenly finds a litter of babies to contend with. More often than not, the baby gerbils are killed and sometimes eaten; once this deplorable habit starts, it is very difficult to stop. A low protein diet also is often blamed as a cause of cannibalism.

Nest boxes are not really a necessity when breeding gerbils. The exception is, of course, in the case of more nervous species. Anything can be used as a nest, as long as it is dry, warm and easily accessible. Budgerigar nest boxes are excellent and can be replaced at little cost if they get damaged by gnawing.

This gerbil is being tamed and taught to eat from the hand with some sunflower seeds. Photo by R. Hanson.

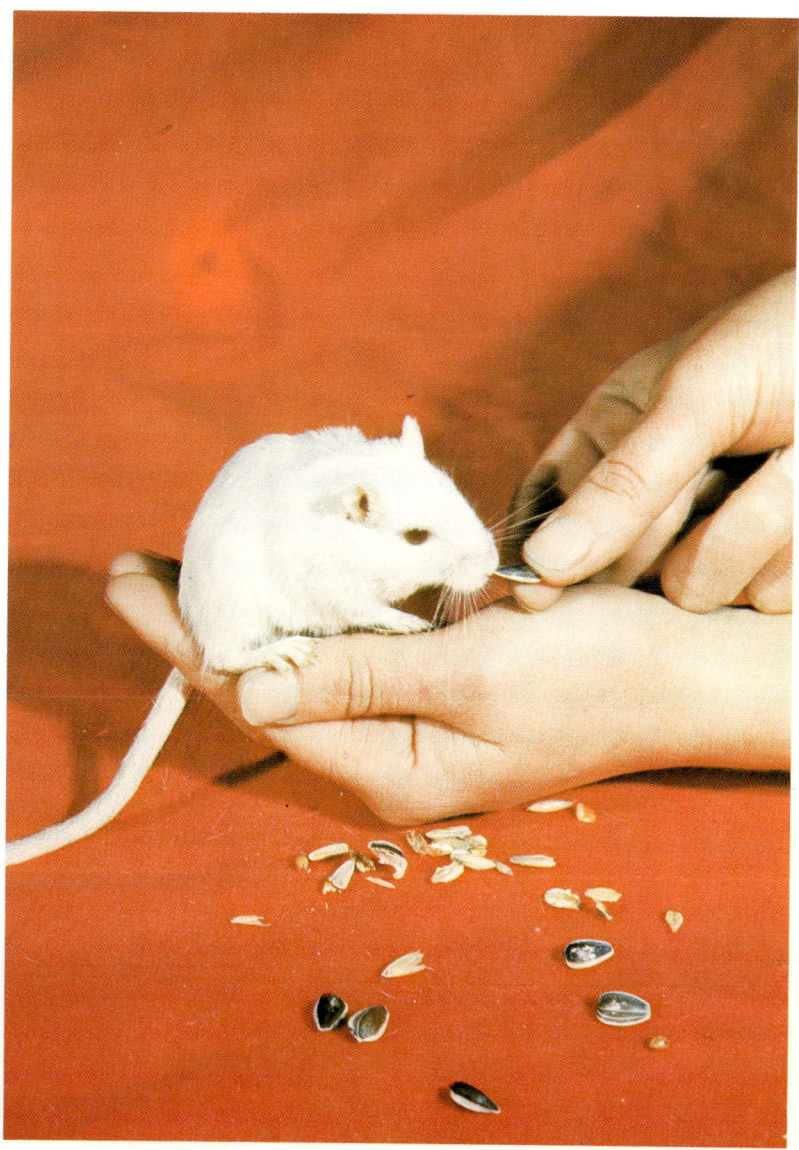

Note how carefully this gerbil is taking a sunflower seed from the fingers. Photo by R. Hanson.

Simple Genetics

Genetics is the science of inheritance, the study of how certain characteristics are passed from one or both parents to their young. The study of genetics has been practiced for many years by professional geneticists all over the world. The basic principles are well understood, but there are controversial areas and aspects also which still elude even the most knowledgeable scientists.

Almost nothing is known of the genetics of gerbils. They are relatively new to the scientific world, and much is yet to be learned about them. For example, since the introduction of the Mongolian gerbil into western Europe and America there have been a number of changes in the natural or wild color. This has been brought about by the fact that since the early days of gerbil breeding large numbers of the species have been bred in captivity. The large-scale breeding has widened the spectrum from which mutations can be produced and increased the chances of mutations. Before going into the details of mutations, it will be easier to explain simply the normal pattern of inheritance.

Each new gerbil that is born is a nearly exact replica of its parents, the usual gerbil characteristics being passed on to it in this way. The inheritance factors from the male are passed on in each particle of his sperm; the female's inheritance factors are contained in the egg that is fertilized by the male sperm. In the human body there are 23 pairs of chromosomes, each sperm and each egg containing only the 23 single chromosomes of these

150

Under ordinary situations one can only expect a progeny of gerbils that are very similar to the wild Mongolian gerbil. Photo by Studio Morgan.

pairs. When they unite, there is a total of 46 chromosomes in the fertilized egg or zygote. Within each chromosome there are large numbers of chemical units termed genes. It is the gene that is actually responsible for whichever inheritance factor that is transmitted.

The young gerbil receives from each of its parents the genes in each of their chromosomes. If the parents of this youngster are pure-bred, that is to say, if they have been bred from a long line of gerbils that are normal in every way, then the chances are that the youngster in question will also be pure-bred and exactly like its parents. The genes carry within them such inheritable characteristics as coat color, eye color and type and texture of fur. It can only receive one of these inheritance

A gerbil caught in the act of "marking" a small piece of wood. This is done by rubbing the surface of the wood with its scent gland, situated on its belly. This is done repeatedly as it scurries back and forth. Photo by R. Hanson.

A family of gerbils shredding a paper towel for a nest. This container is obviously not large enough to house so many gerbils; removal of all others except the breeding pair is advised. Photo by R. Hanson.

These photos show the big difference in the size and appearance between one-day-old gerbils (above) and the same gerbils one week later. Photo by D.G. Robinson, Jr.

factors from each adult because the genes move in a set pattern which is referred to as the Mendelian laws of heredity. Of the pair of genes it receives, that which shows itself in the young gerbil's appearance is known as the dominant gene.

This can be explained further by taking a typical example. If a normally colored (technically called Agouti) gerbil is mated to a white gerbil, the young that are produced will be all Agouti-colored. However, latent within their genetic make-up they will still possess the gene that produces white fur. The white gene does not show itself within the first generation because the Agouti gene is dominant and completely masks it. The white gene is, therefore, termed recessive and the young gerbil produced by this cross is termed an Agouti that is recessive for white. In the study of genetics, each identified gene for a particular color or other character is given a letter to signify its properties. The dominant gene is always given a capital letter. In the gerbil the Agouti gene is written as "A"; when applied to the purebred Agouti gerbil the symbol "AA" is used, indicating that one A gene was received from *each* parent (A + A = AA).

The white gerbil bred from white parents for many generations is distinguished by the symbol "cc." Capital letters are not used here because the white gene is recessive to all others. The young produced from the first mating of Agouti and white will be Agouti in color but not purebred Agouti as one parent was white. The genetical symbols used for each of these young gerbils will be "Ac" showing that the gerbil is Agouti-colored but carries the white factor.

If we now venture further and mate a pair of young gerbils that each have Agouti and white parents, the result will be slightly different. It is probable that in the progeny from a series of such matings in the long run

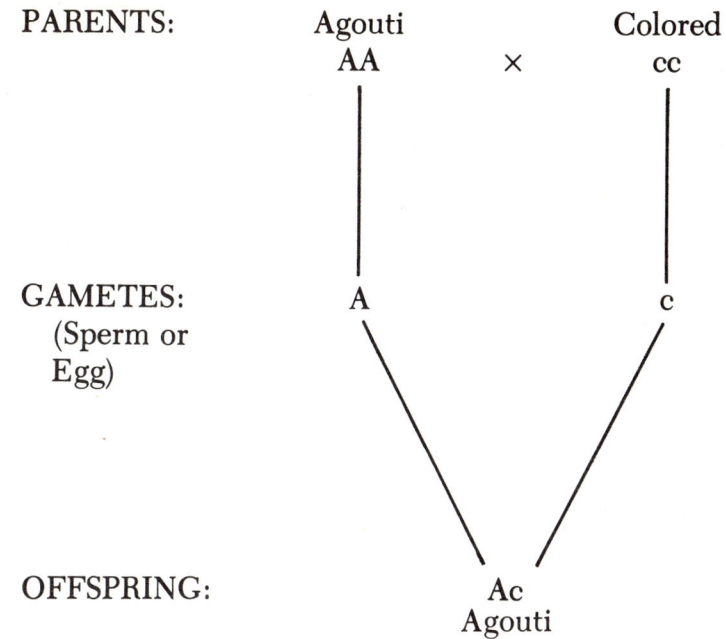

PARENTS: Agouti   Colored

AA   ×   cc

GAMETES: A   c
(Sperm or
Egg)

OFFSPRING: Ac
Agouti

Diagram of the inheritance of a dominant gene **A** and a recessive gene **c** in an Agouti and a white gerbil cross.

to expect pure bred Agouti (AA), impure Agouti (Ac) and pure white (cc). The ratio of colors produced in this way should be three Agouti to one white. As explained earlier, the purebred Agouti would receive both of the dominant "A" genes from its parents. The impure Agouti would receive one of each type of gene and will, therefore, have the same make-up as their parents. The white gerbil on the other hand, would receive a recessive from each of its parents and because there is no dominant gene, the white color is able to be seen.

Of course, the more the gerbils are interbred the more combinations of genes are possible. Along with color-carrying genes, there are also others which determine the shape and height or length of the body, the length of the tail and so on; these genes generally work in exactly the same way as the genes for color, although

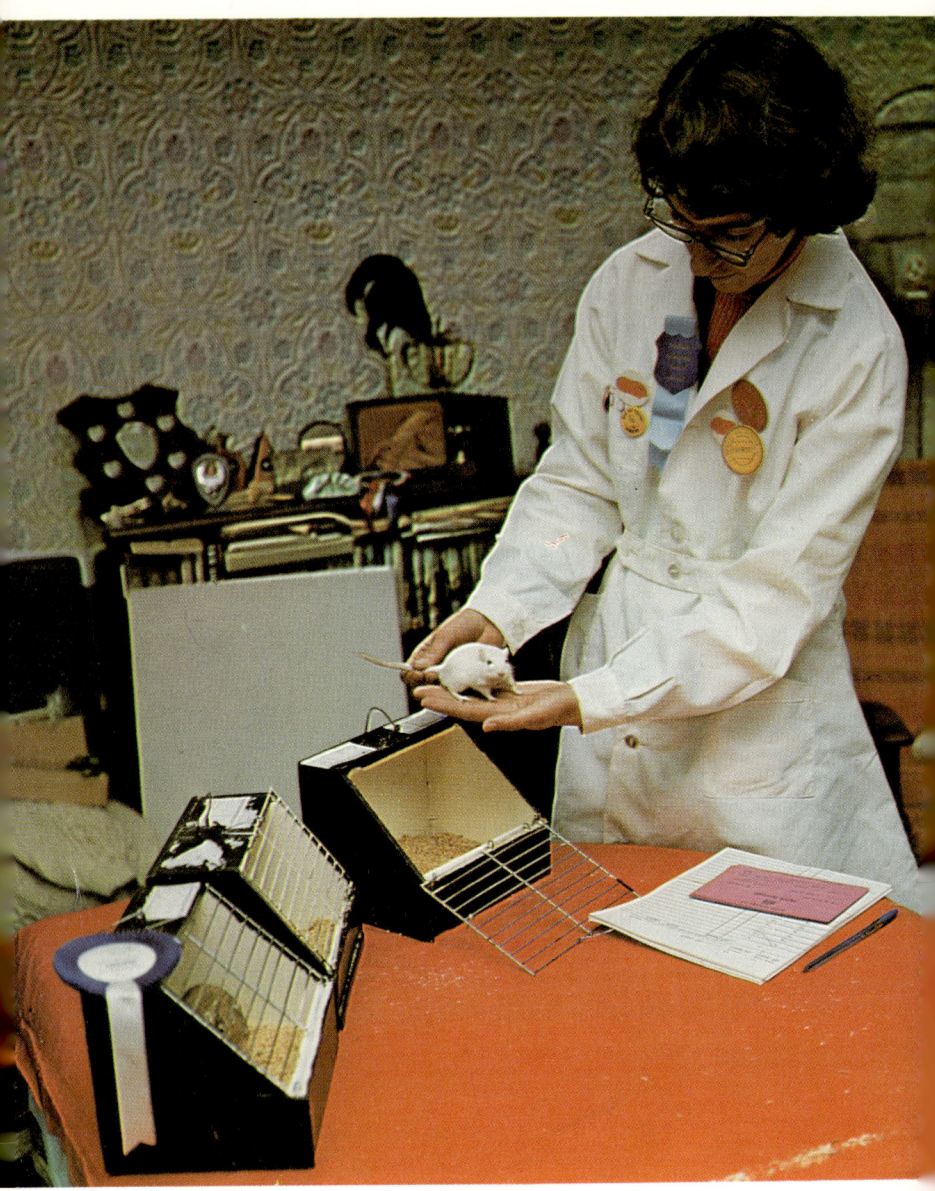

Time for showing, and a qualified judge is assessing the finer points of a white gerbil. Points are noted on a printed form. Photo by R. Hanson.

Appearance of a normal Mongolian gerbil showing the agouti color pattern. Photo by Ray Hanson.

A white gerbil, one of the known mutations in gerbils.

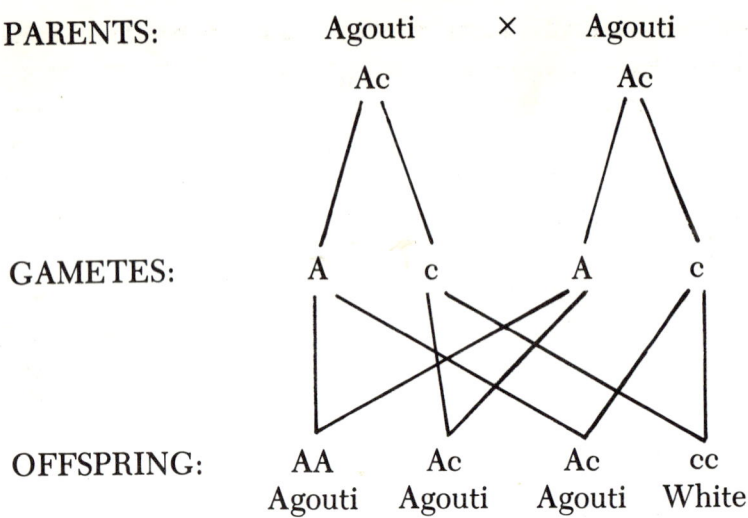

PARENTS: Agouti   ×   Agouti
                Ac   Ac

GAMETES: A   c   A   c

OFFSPRING: AA   Ac   Ac   cc
             Agouti Agouti Agouti White

Diagram of the inheritance of Agouti and white genes from hybrid Agouti parents.

in many cases the rules for determining the genetic nature of the offspring are more complex and difficult to understand.

A mutant is a living creature that is different from the normal in one way or another. The genes change slightly to produce the mutant. More often than not, it is the recessive genes that do this. This can also be better explained by returning to color. When an Agouti male is mated to an Agouti female, it sometimes happens that the gene for color pigmentation is completely missing. In such an accident, a gerbil that appears pure white in color will eventually be produced; the eyes of such an animal will be pink and red, the toenails and ears flesh-colored. (In the absence of any pigmentation, the light that strikes the gerbil's eyes will produce the pink color, since the blood vessels within the eye are illuminated. The same applies to the toenails and the ears, although to a lesser extent.) However, the genes that produce this animal or mutant are recessive and therefore do not show themselves in the first generation; it is only when two recessive genes combine that the full extent of the mutation is visible. The combination can only be produced when two gerbils of the same parentage—each carrying the same genes—are by chance mated together. Very often a mutation is produced and lost because of the fact that it is not visible at once. The gerbil carrying the mutant gene is mated to another that carries both dominant genes; therefore the effects of the recessive mutant gene will not be visible, rather than showing up once in every four offspring if two mutants are mated.

Mutations are not noticed as often in the wild as they are in captivity. If wild gerbils were to produce a white gerbil, its chances of survival in the wild would be slim. Being different in color from others of its kind, it would be more noticeable and, therefore, an easy target for a predator. Also, it might be unable to attract a mate.

The chances of such a mutation being produced in the wild are also lessened by the fact that when the mutant gene originally appears it is normally masked in the first generation. The chances of this gerbil mating with another gerbil that carries the same set of genes are fairly remote, so too, in fact, is the occurrence of a gene that produces a change in the normal shape of a gerbil. If a gerbil was born with extremely short hind legs, for instance, the chances of it mating with another gerbil with the same short legs would not be high. Of course, it does sometimes happen that such a feature as short hind legs becomes fixed in the next generation when the parent mates with another gerbil of the same family. But the resulting young gerbils would not be fast enough to escape their natural enemies; in this way natural selection ensures that the fittest of the species survive. If

It will not be unusual if these white gerbils at a later stage should develop a few dark hairs at the tail. Photo by Ray Hanson.

In this position the separation between the darker (agouti) upper part and the pale ventral part of the coat of a gerbil is distinctly shown. Photo by D.G. Robinson, Jr.

such a mutation is favorable to survive, then it is likely to stay.

Occasional mutations are dominant and thus visible in the first generation. These are of course usually easier to fix if worthwhile.

Throughout this chapter there has been mention of a white gerbil and it is common knowledge that nearly all white animals, including human beings, with pink eyes are known as albinos. There are, in fact, two kinds of albinos: the complete albino, where there is no color pigmentation at all, and the partial albino, where small amounts of pigmentation exist. The white or albino gerbil belongs to the latter group because it is not a com-

The Himalayan color pattern is found in many mammals, such as cats, rabbits, rats, mice and hamsters. The pattern is easily recognized by the points (dark areas on the feet, tail, snout and ears), as seen in one of these hamsters.

Unlike gerbils, guinea pigs have been domesticated for centuries, giving breeders a chance to produce more coat and color varieties. Photo by H.V. Lacey.

plete albino. While it is still young, and indeed up to three months of age, the white gerbil does appear to be completely albino. After this age, however, the tail begins to show markings of dark brown hairs, showing that the gerbil is an incomplete albino. This type of albinism is termed Himalayan: the body is pure white but the nose, ears, tail and/or feet are marked. It will be

The capability of gerbils to produce a uniform and healthy progeny is already established, but their breeding performance is still not predictable. Photo by Studio Morgan.

noticed that these points are the extremities of the animal's body. These parts of the body lose heat more quickly than the other, and it has been found that the colder these parts are, the deeper the color that is present on them. Himalayan albinism can be seen in the cat, mouse, guinea pig and, to a lesser extent, hamster. In the first three animals all the points are colored, but in the hamster it is only the ears that are colored. The gerbil follows more or less the same pattern as the hamster in that only one part, the tail, is colored. The Himalayan gerbil mutation, first produced in England in 1968, has become very popular and is still on the increase.

It is not unreasonable to expect more mutations to occur affecting any character of a gerbil. Fanciers especially would like to produce gerbils quite different from the typical one shown. Photo by D. G. Robinson, Jr.

Mutants can appear at any time and at any place. The importance of such discoveries is not often realized because they arise by accident and the owner looks upon the strange gerbil as a mere freak. Very often it is kept as a curiosity and never bred from, so the mutation is lost, perhaps forever. Since the discovery of the white gerbil a number of other mutations of great importance has been produced. The second color mutation to appear was that of silver; this one was bred in the United States, but little has been heard of it since. The silver-colored gerbil was bred by a Mr. Meares, and pictures of it appeared in various gerbil publications around that time in 1969; the booklet *Enjoy your Gerbils* contained a picture of this color.

The third mutation to reach prominence was bred in Canada. It was a gerbil of the normal Agouti color but which sported white patches on the forehead, the nape of the neck and the feet. The first specimens were imported to England in 1968 and were at the time termed "Canadian White Spots." The mutation was almost lost until an interested breeder took up the challenge and started to breed large numbers of the mutation but not without great difficulty. It was at first thought that the amount of white could be increased by mating this mutation to a white gerbil. This was not to be, however, because all that was produced were gerbils that carried exactly the same amount of white.

It should be mentioned that there seems some possibility of modifying color genes of the gerbil. These genes are in simple terms mixing genes. Their action has the effect of diluting the Agouti color when mixed with white. The amount of dilution has only a limited effect, and once a certain degree of dilution has been reached there is no further advancement. This is partly speculation, but it does happen in this way with the rabbit. Here the modifying genes are present in the sable color and, depending on the amount present, the modifying genes give a sable of light, medium or dark shading.

Perhaps the most exciting discovery made so far is that of the black mutation of the Mongolian gerbil. This mutation was discovered by scientists at the U.S.A.F. School of Aerospace Medicine in Texas. The mutation was produced from Agouti-colored gerbils. At first only one such animal was born, but it was only a matter of

A male agouti gerbil and its white mate. Unless this male is a carrier of white factor, the expected litter should resemble the male. Photos by Studio Morgan.

time before other individuals were reared. The black gerbil is not entirely black in color; it has a white line running from underneath the chin along the stomach. In England, one or two other mutants have appeared that are gray in color, but the full potential of this mutation has yet to be reached.

Mutations are generally established in quantity by inbreeding rather than by other means of selective breeding. In simple terms, inbreeding is the mating together of related stock—as opposed to crossbreeding, the mating together of unrelated stock. Almost all exhibition animals are produced by inbreeding. This has

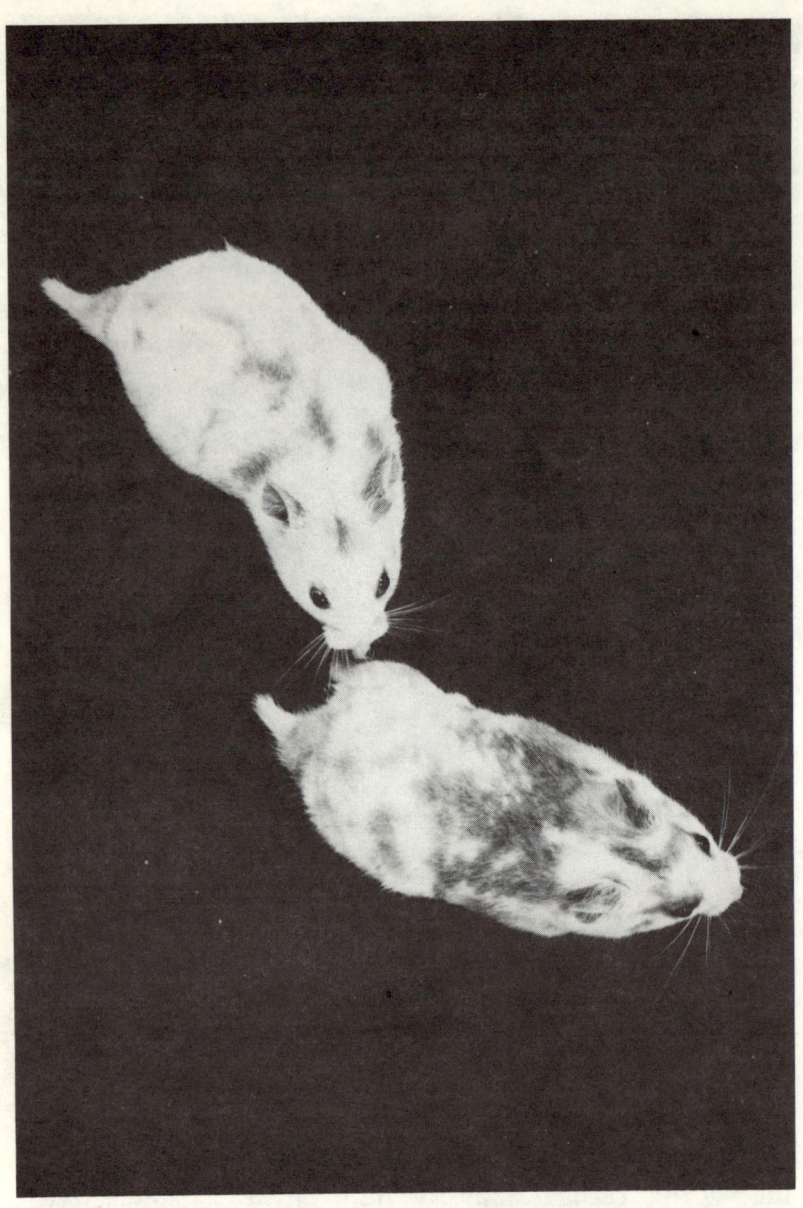

Piebald or random spotted pattern is not unusual in the hamster (above) and other mammals. The mutation has appeared in the gerbil, but it is still very rare. Photo by M. Roberts.

It will take some time before gerbils can equal the types of mutations that are known in the mouse (about six varieties are recognizable above). Photo by T.A. Mazzarello.

A room with rows of stacked cages for breeding hamsters commercially; this type of arrangement is quite appropriate for gerbils also.

the advantage of fixing selected good points within the animals. However, it can also fix bad points just as easily and should be practiced with caution. From what has already been said about how the mutant gene is transmitted, it can be seen that inbreeding helps to fix it because the mutant gene is further strengthened by breeding back to the gerbil that carries it in its genetic makeup. When the mutation is fixed it is strengthened and shows its presence by appearing in more and more animals. If inbreeding is practiced, gerbils from the same litter are usually mated together and thus the mutation is preserved.

For economic reasons commercial breeders rarely give their gerbils
fresh green food. Water and pellet type food (the same kind given to
mice and rats) are provided. Photo by Dr. H.R. Axelrod.

The inexperienced breeder is often at a loss when he realizes that a new color is present within the stock. In such a case, the guidance of a geneticist should be sought. If one is not available, the best course of action is to select a male from the litter and mate it back to its mother; similarly, a young female should be selected from the same litter and mated back to its father. From these matings there is every chance that the new color will show itself even more clearly. Of course, complications can occur if the gerbils are kept in colonies since the exact parentage may be in some doubt, and it will require a lot of patient inbreeding before the source of the mutant gene is ascertained.

Ailments and First Aid

Almost all species of gerbil are very clean in their habits. This makes them easy to look after since any mess that they do make is kept to a neat minimum. A dirty cage, however, is a breeding ground for all types of disease, and cleaning out should be done often. It goes without saying that dirty gerbils cannot be healthy.

Although gerbils are rodents, they are not known to carry and transmit as many diseases as other rodents, particularly the rat. All rodents though are known to be transmitters of the deadly disease of rabies. In Western countries there are strict rules and regulations which control the number and quality of animals imported, and the animals must spend a specified amount of time in quarantine when they arrive. The period of quarantine gives the animal time to show any disease that it might be carrying at the time of and just after entry. In this way the spread of such diseases as rabies is brought under control. Imported gerbils offered for sale in pet stores and by animal dealers have served the quarantine period and are all certified to be free from any health hazard to the general public. In Egypt, however, with laxer laws, the Libyan gerbil has been blamed for the spread of schistosomiasis, a high infectious blood fluke that probably affects over half the population.

Gerbils that are housed and fed properly will very rarely fall victim to any kind of serious illness, and they should remain healthy and active all their lives. Gerbils are very hardy and do not suffer from anything beyond the scope of even an inexperienced owner. However, minor ailments that cannot be foreseen by even the expert sometimes strike at the most unexpected moment. The keeper who knows his stock thoroughly will be able to spot any such ailments right from the moment that they appear. The healthy gerbil is alert, bright-eyed and never stands still for very long. Its fur is sleek and shiny; it is clean and never badly stained in any way. The gerbil's signs of ill health are obvious; he will sit in a corner, his fur will be ruffled and dull, his eyes also dull and sullen and he will not be interested in anything going on around him. A diseased animal should be kept for further development. Usually all that is required to clear up the trouble is the administration of a simple antibiotic. For example, should a gerbil be suffering from nothing more harmful than a common cold, the application of an aromatic oil such as eucalyptus will quickly help to clear the nuisance. Also, in the case of injuries, it is a simple matter to apply an antiseptic preparation to the wounds. If a time comes, however, when the gerbil owner is at a loss, he should of course get the advice of a vet.

Remember too your own health! Everyone at some time or another gets nipped by his animals unless they are extremely docile, and it is common sense to protect yourself against any complication that might develop from a gerbil bite. The chances of real trouble are slim, but if you like, you can arrange for your family doctor to give an anti-tetanus injection. It is too late if the bite turns septic—and a course of such injections are cheap at double the price!

COLDS

Colds are perhaps the most common of all animal complaints. An afflicted gerbil will be constantly sneezing, the eyes may run and the nose may be wet. In some cases a lack of appetite is evident and the gerbil appears

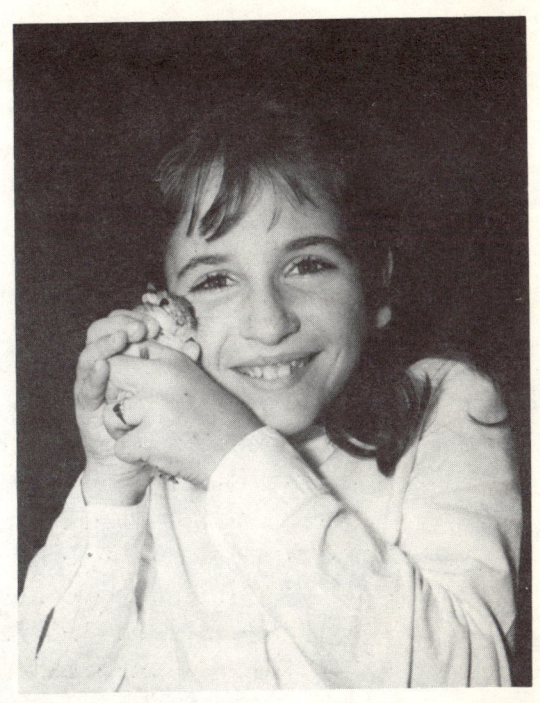

It is best not to place a gerbil close to one's face. Gerbils can bite, and possible infection can ensue. Lower photo by Studio Morgan, upper photo by Dr. H.R. Axelrod.

Normal activity (mostly play) is characteristic of gerbils, but frenetic activity could be an indication of illness and should not be ignored. Photo by D.G. Robinson, Jr.

lethargic. Colds and chills are usually caused by crowded, drafty or damp conditions. The easiest remedy is to remove the conditions that give rise to infection, block up any drafts and ensure that the cage is kept dry and warm.

Remove some of the gerbils too if you feel that there are too many for the amount of available cage space. Colds are contagious, and any animal that is suffering should be isolated as early as possible. It should be put in a warm airy room and left for nature to do the rest. The gerbil can be made comfortable by dabbing a piece of cotton soaked in eucalyptus oil around its nose. This will not bring a miracle cure, but it will loosen any mucus that may have hardened within the nasal passages; the oil gives off a vapor that inhibits the mucus-producing glands and ensures that the nose is kept free. Once the cold has run its course, recovery is rapid and the patient will soon be back to its normal self. Colds can be avoided to some extent by the regular use of cod liver oil as an additive to the diet. The fish oil does not actually fight a cold, but it strengthens the body to resist germs.

DIARRHEA

Injudicious feeding is usually the cause of diarrhea. As bad or spoiled foods are usually the culprits, a constant watch should be kept to ensure that nothing rotten or otherwise unsuitable is fed to the gerbils. The symptoms of diarrhea are unmistakable; the gerbil will leave a mess whenever it does its toilet and the offensive smell will tell the gerbil owner all he needs to know.

Diarrhea can sometimes be passed on to other gerbils, so action should be taken at once to avoid an epidemic. Any gerbils so afflicted should be separated and fed only dry rations. Green food should be withheld and not offered again until the condition has been com-

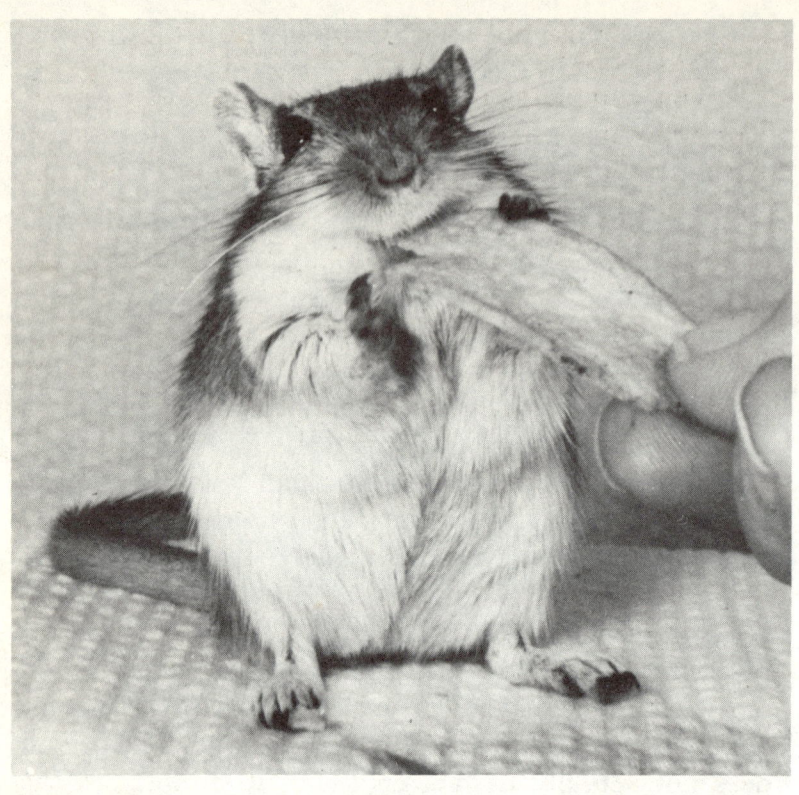

Corn in the form of chips or flakes is utilized more efficiently than in an unprocessed or whole grain form. Tempting your gerbil with corn chips is quite permissible. Photo by D.G. Robinson, Jr.

pletely eliminated. When the diarrhea is severe, a pinch of powdered arrowroot should be added to the dry food. If this is unobtainable, then a small piece of arrowroot biscuit can be offered. A return to normal should take place within 48 hours after the arrowroot has been fed. If the gerbils seem to be no better, take the advice of a vet.

The cages and feeding utensils should be washed out in hot water with a tablespoon of household ammonia added. If the outbreak is very severe, it is wise to wash the cage as well; it should be left to dry out for at least twenty-four hours before the gerbils are put back.

CONSTIPATION

This complaint is very rarely encountered, but it does sometimes effect gerbils. The cause is not usually due to feeding when the normal diet is fed, but if unnatural foods such as chocolate and other sweet things have been eaten they can have a binding effect.

More often than not, however, gerbils become constipated by chewing and swallowing their own bedding. This is particularly true if cotton wool or other fibrous materials are used. The gerbil eats minute pieces of wool and in time they accumulate in the intestine and can cause a blockage. The symptoms are not easy to observe unless the cage is clean. Then complete absence of droppings should be enough to cause the gerbil owner to suspect something amiss.

Fine fibrous materials like cotton have no place in a gerbil's cage; if ingested, cotton could form balls and block the digestive tube.

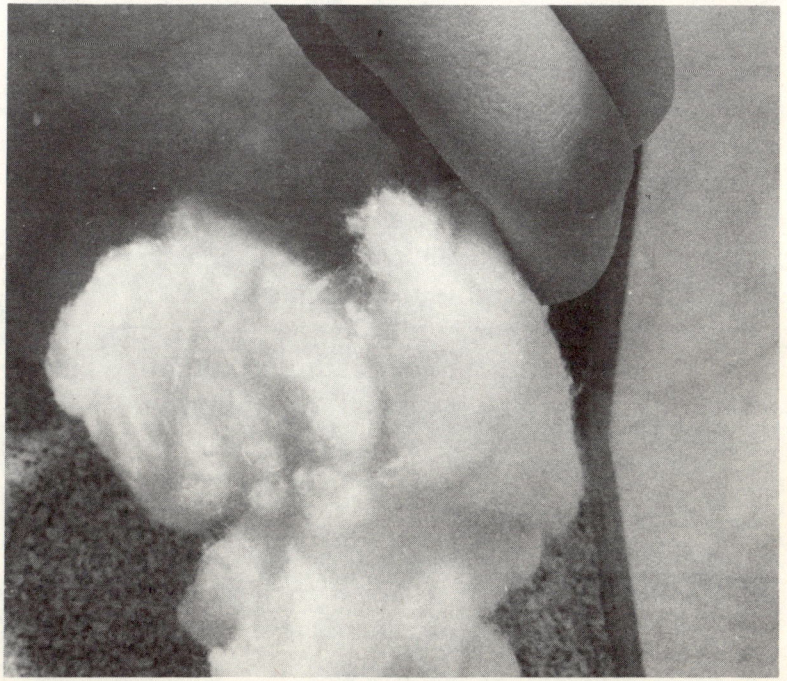

The long-term effects of such an intestinal blockage are very serious indeed. The stomach becomes inflated and the rear end of the gerbil will bulge. In very serious cases the stomach may even rupture; in such an event death soon follows.

Action should be taken as soon as the condition is suspected. All bedding should immediately be replaced with something that has already been shredded. Coarse cotton or sacking is ideal. Change the normal diet to one that contains plenty of green foods; if milk is offered instead of the more usual water, this may prove beneficial in prompting the gerbil's bowels to move. The use of castor oil should be limited to emergency use only. It has very drastic effects and should be used with great caution. One single drop mixed with the food is sufficient to treat one or two gerbils. When it becomes clear these remedies are taking effect, their use should be discontinued.

EYE INFECTIONS

Gerbils are famous for their ability to dig deep into sand. In order to protect their eyes from foreign matter they have a very thin second eyelid known as the nictitating membrane. It is a transparent membrane only one-thousandth of an inch thick which moves so fast that it is almost invisible to human eyesight.

Accidents do sometimes happen, and particles of sand can become trapped beneath the nictitating membrane and set up a severe irritation. In its efforts to dislodge the offending matter, the gerbil very often causes serious damage to the eye. It has sometimes happened that gerbils have completely scratched out the eyeball. Should this ever happen, there is nothing that can be done, and it is more humane to destroy the gerbil painlessly. Constant scratching is a tell-tale sign that a gerbil has eye trouble. The area around the eye also

A gerbil in the process of "burrowing" into the bedding. With this behavior in mind, one realizes the necessity of using a type of bedding material which should not injure the eyes. Photo by D.G. Robinson, Jr.

becomes inflamed and devoid of fur.

In these circumstances you must help the gerbil by bathing its eye. Use a *soft* paint brush, such as are used in children's paint sets. Dip the brush in warm water and, carrying a lot of water, very gently drip it across the top of the eye. As the water runs down it should take the sand with it, but just in case the eye is not completely clear, it should be bathed every hour or so. Never be tempted to poke at the eyeball in any way, for more permanent damage will be caused.

A tunnel-like system of whatever sort will always be used. However, paper materials will not last very long. Photo by D.G. Robinson, Jr.

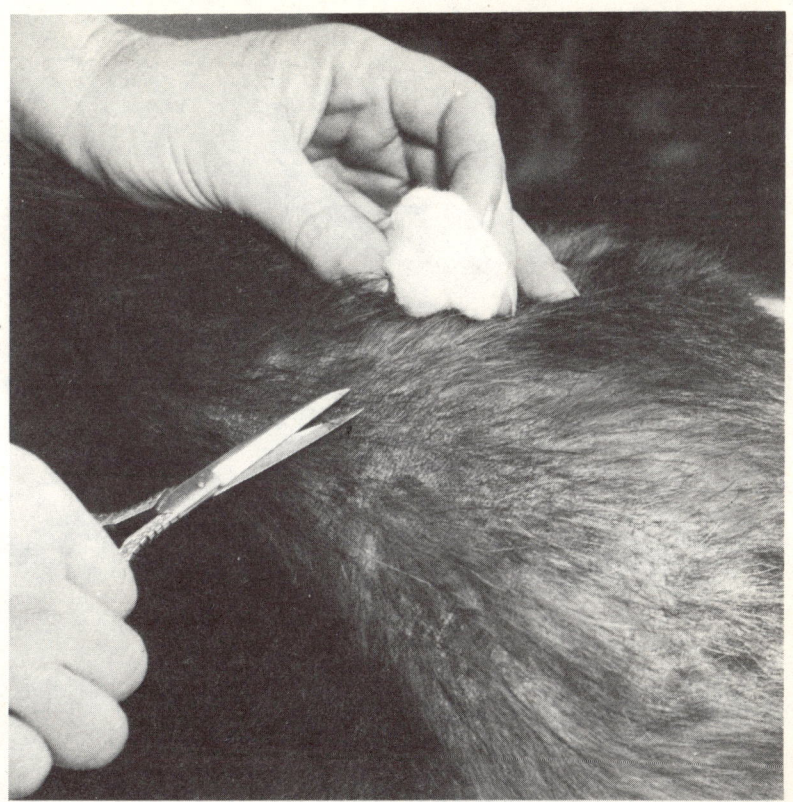

Mange is easy to recognize in most pet mammals, such as the dog shown here above. In both the wet or dry types bald patches are symptomatic of the disease. Photo by L. van der Meid.

MANGE

There are two main types of mange that affect gerbils. The infection can be introduced by a new gerbil, and every new arrival should be thoroughly inspected for signs of disease.

Wet mange can be detected as soon as it is contracted. Small papules or blisters appear on the hind quarters, feet and ears. These pimple-like eruptions begin to ooze fluid and quickly turns into sores. The fur around the affected area begins to fall away until there is nothing left but big bald patches.

A gerbil surrounded by an array of food that will keep it healthy and free from the usual nutritional deficiencies.

Dry mange is not as easily diagnosed in its early stages. The fur falls gradually, especially around the hindquarters, and the exposed skin is very dry and flakes away.

Mange in any variety is very contagious, and any infected animal should be isolated well away from the other gerbils. In mange, vitamin C is often lacking and citrus fruit such as. oranges should be given to combat the deficiency. A whole orange can be offered or the gerbil's water can be replaced by diluted orange juice. This should be continued until the condition appears to be clearing up, and even then the orange juice can be added to the ordinary drinking water to ensure the continued presence of vitamin C in the diet. The fur and skin should be treated with a commercial mange preparation according to the instructions until the fur begins to regain its natural growth and density.

Gerbils that have the misfortune of being allowed the use of an exercise wheel often have fur loss also, especially evident along the back and rump. Remove the wheel—permanently if possible—and rub a small amount of zinc and castor oil ointment on the affected area. Do not be impatient; the growth of new fur may

The potential danger of an exercise wheel cannot be ignored; tail deformities (kinked tails), loss of fur and even amputated tails are some effects of its use. Photo by D.G. Robinson, Jr.

be rather slow at first. Once the wheel has been removed, it will give the fur a better chance to regain its original length.

Do not be tempted to breed from a gerbil which has had mange. The disease being contagious, the litter will be very vulnerable and its spread will have catastrophic effects.

Gerbils that have mange should be tended only *after* you have attended to the healthy stock. Take care after feeding the gerbils to wash your hands thoroughly. Any infection of other gerbils (and other animals too) is restricted if these simple rules are followed.

PARASITES

A parasite is an animal that lives on another. Internal parasites enter the body usually through the mouth; the external parasites live close to the skin of animals but do not enter the body.

The internal parasite is picked up by animals—and sometimes man himself—in the form of its eggs or larvae, usually through contaminated food. The eggs of such parasites travel within the body of the host and attach themselves to various organs; the larvae nourish themselves on the semi-digested matter that is the animal's own food. Some types of internal parasite feed on the host's blood and other chemicals vital to the animal's well-being. The result of this is that the animal cannot grow to its full potential and therefore falls easy prey to all kinds of minor ailments.

Worms are the most common of all internal parasites, and they are usually picked up from infected green foods. All green food should therefore be thoroughly washed before being fed to your gerbils. The worm itself hatches out within the body from an egg that has been swallowed; when it reaches maturity it lays another batch of eggs. The adult worms are often

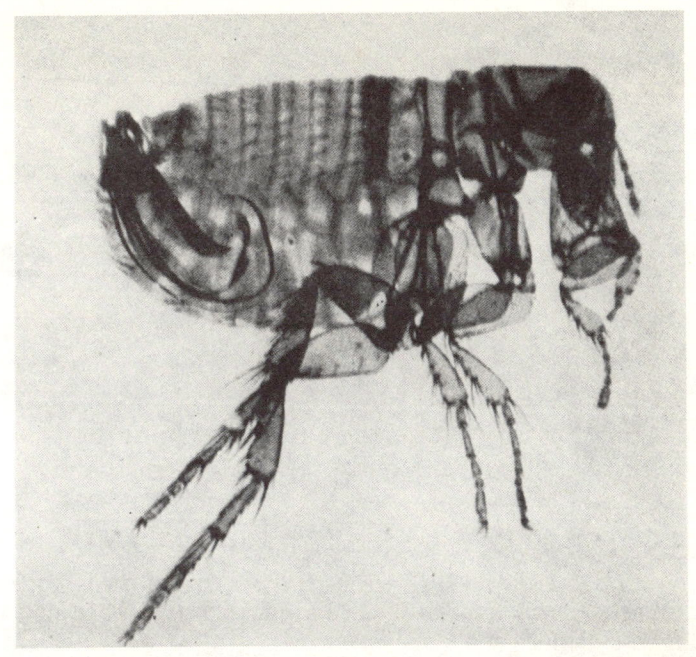

Enlarged photographs of fleas (male and female). Note the six pairs and two feelers which are some of the characteristic features of insects. Photo courtesy of the American Museum of Natural History.

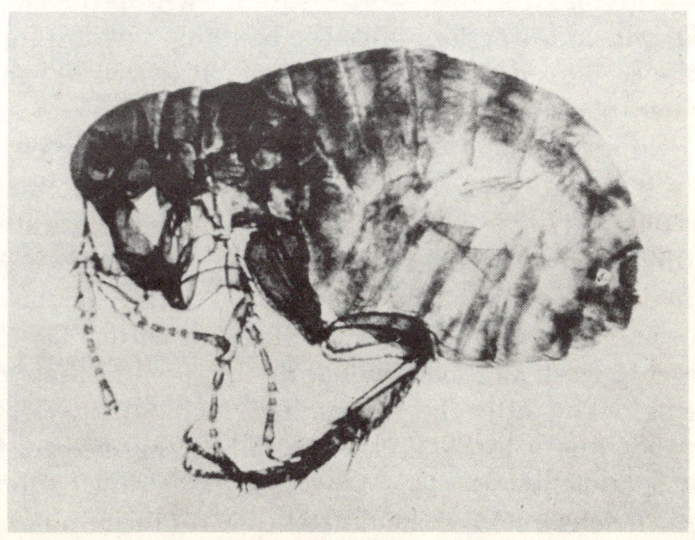

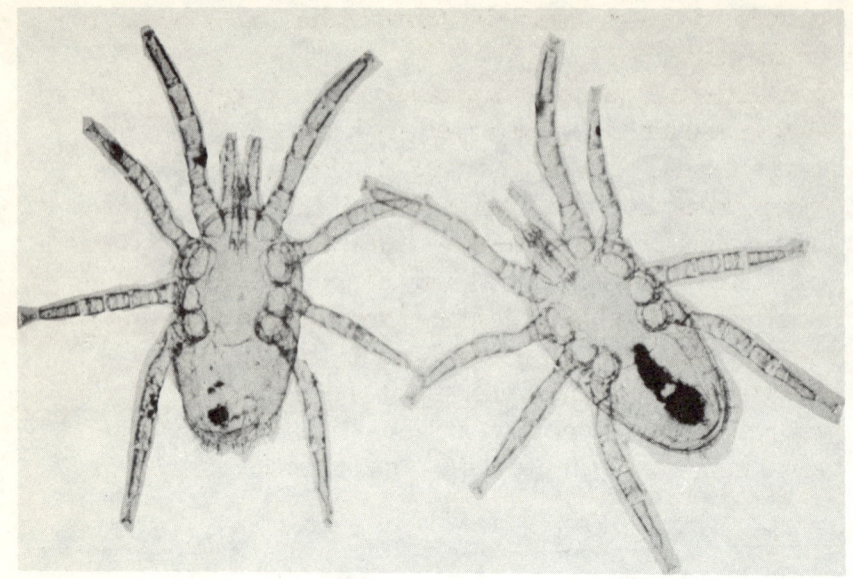

Typical appearance of mites. Mites are arachnids (related to spiders) and have eight legs and lack feelers.

excreted with the feces along with quantities of the eggs. Other gerbils become infected by taking in these eggs.

The mere expulsion of the worm may be enough to kill a gerbil. If such a worm is found within the cage, take immediate action; burn the bedding, sawdust and, if the gerbil is dead, its body as well. It is wise to run a lighted blowtorch over all the surfaces of the cage. If you do not want to risk running the paint of the cage, take it outside and find a bowl large enough to completely receive the cage. Fill the tub with boiling water, adding to it a strong antiseptic such as carbolic acid. Leave the cage in this solution until the water begins to cool and then thoroughly rinse it in hot water. Do not forget to wash all food bowls and other utensils that you use in looking after the gerbils. This includes any cleaning tools and brushes. Only when all this has been done can it be considered safe to return the gerbils to their cage. A constant vigil should be kept over the remaining gerbils to ensure that the parasite has been properly eradicated.

External parasites are rarely seen on gerbils; they can, however, be transferred from other animals that carry them. The most common of these pests include red mites, fleas and lice. Red mites are tiny red creatures about the size of a pinhead. They live close to the skin, and their food is fresh blood, hence their color. The common flea, which infests pet dogs and cats, is almost certainly too large to live on gerbils—luckily for them!

Lice are common parasites. They live in the fur of the animal but do not fly or jump. Incessant biting and scratching of the fur are indications that the gerbil is be-

Extreme caution should be exercised when using tick and flea powders on gerbils. Discontinue the medication as soon as any unusual reaction is observed.

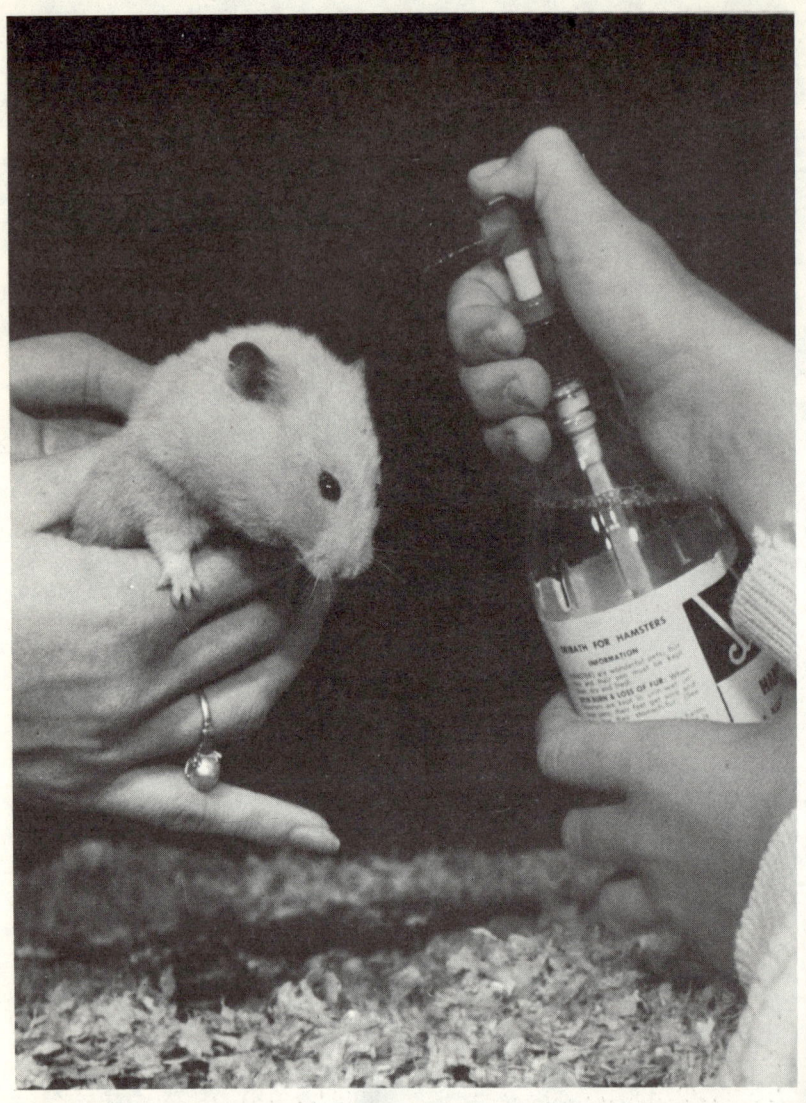

The same caution should be considered in the application of liquid pesticides (even one that is intended for hamsters seen above). Photo by L. van der Meid.

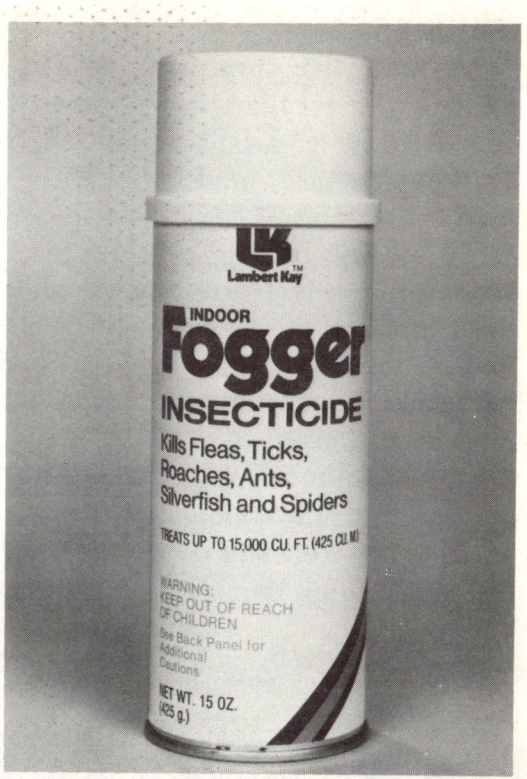

A room should not be sprayed with insecticides while gerbils are in it; potent insecticides can kill them easily.

ing troubled by such pests. To treat them, remove the gerbil from its cage and dust it with a good flea powder. It is better to use a powder that is sold for use on cats and small animals; dog flea powders are too strong and can cause inflammation. Make sure the powder gets well into the fur and leave it for 20 to 30 minutes. When the powder has had time to do its work, rub or brush it out. Be careful that the eyes are covered during the dusting operation. Repeat the dusting 24 hours later. After this time the gerbil should be free from any kind of external parasites. The cage bedding and floor dressing should be burned and the whole of the inside of the cage dusted with powder. When fresh bedding and floor dressing are put in, it is a wise precaution to mix some of the flea powder in with them.

INJURIES

Gerbils that suffer from serious injuries are better treated by a vet than in the home.

Fighting and falls are two of the most common sources of injuries, and both can be prevented if common sense is used. Whenever a gerbil is handled, it should always be held over a table so that if it should slip it will not be injured. Never allow children to handle a gerbil without supervision. A child's intentions are loving, but if a gerbil is held tightly serious injury may be caused. There is also the obvious danger that a child may be bitten.

Broken limbs are very difficult to set. A gerbil will not keep still long enough for a broken bone to heal. Any dressing or splint will be immediately chewed away. If the broken limb hangs loosely, the break is a clean one

Beware of leaving gerbils with larger animals, even an apparently tame pet rabbit; the latter can pounce and maim a tiny gerbil. Photo by Studio Morgan.

A miniature spinning wheel like this should not pose much danger to gerbils. Photo by Studio Morgan.

and the limb is made useless; there is little chance of such a fracture healing to its former shape. Any such injury causes much pain and it is more humane to have the gerbil put to sleep. Minor breaks will heal satisfactorily if left alone. These fractures are usually of the "greenstick" nature, where the bone splinters instead of breaks.

Cuts and wounds can be caused by bites from other gerbils and by sharp projections within the cage. A plaster or gauze pad is of little use—the gerbil will merely chew it away. Dab the wound instead with a pad soaked in a mild antiseptic and leave it alone. The wound should heal quickly and leave no trace of a scar. In instances where the cut is a deep one, there may be loss of fur, and this should be accepted. There is nothing that can be done to make the hair grow again.

If a wound turns septic, you should get the advice of a vet. Never meddle with any medicines that you are not sure about; you are more likely to damage than improve your gerbil's health in this way. Remember, in all cases of first aid prevention is much better than cure.

FITS

There has been recent note of the gerbil's susceptibility to what appears as fits. In fact, the condition is not an illness as such but rather a state of nervousness.

The Mongolian gerbil when out of the cage will

A gerbil should not be left hanging by its tail without support. Being a very active animal, it will certainly struggle, which could result in some injury to the tail. Photo by Dr. H.R. Axelrod.

often stand on its owner's hand and go into a type of trance. During these trances the whole body trembles slightly. The condition lasts a mere second or two and may never be noticed.

It has been suggested that a lack of vitamin B may cause this. However, gerbils fed on a perfectly balanced diet can also succumb so this does not seem a complete explanation. The Mongolian gerbil often relieves tension by drumming on the ground with its hind feet. There is a possibility that the fit is related to this behavior. Present research does not yet give an answer to this problem.

CANNIBALISM

This is not a recognized disease, but it is certainly worth mentioning because some gerbils have this unpleasant tendency.

This is unfortunately manifested when there are young gerbils only a few days old in the nest. Cannibalism does not appear to follow any pattern. Some females are unable to rear a litter of young because, for one reason or another, they kill and eat all their babies. Some may eat the whole litter in one go, while others will do it one at a time over a period of perhaps a week. Furthermore, others do not eat the complete body but only half, leaving the rest lying about in the cage. It is notable that if the female is a bad mother she will often pass this trait to her surviving daughters. So, only good mothers should be bred from. The male is sometimes responsible also.

It has been found that if gerbils are left short of food for any period of time, those that die are often eaten by their surviving companions. This may perhaps be natural behavior when an animal is starving.

If cannibalism occurs time after time with a pair, first remove the male to find which of the adults is responsible. If the female then rears her litter with no trouble, it will be the male of the pair which is the culprit. There could be several reasons for his actions. Firstly, he could be an adult male that has never before been the father of a litter. Secondly, he may resent the presence of the young within his territory and dispose of them the only way he knows how. Thirdly, it has been suggested that a dietary deficiency could be the cause of his actions.

Vitamin deficiency has been suggested as a cause of all cases of cannibalism. The author cannot follow such reasoning, even though a diet lacking in protein would be corrected by eating flesh. Other reasons for cannibalism such as stress seem more likely. Such a condition can provoke a highly nervous female to destroy her litter rather than have it disturbed and handled by human hands. It is, therefore, of great importance that newborn litters be inspected as soon as they are born and the young counted. They should never be handled or touched in any way. All that is required is to part the nest with a pencil and inspect and count the whole litter. Further disturbance should be kept to an absolute minimum—though this is not always easy when you are trying to ascertain exactly when a cannibalistic female is eating her young.

Environmental circumstances causing anxiety can also be another cause of cannibalism. If the gerbils are kept in the house, the mere presence of the family cat can be enough to send a female to the brink of a nervous breakdown. The result is that her litter is the first to suffer. The same applies to gerbils that are kept in a situation where mice or rats are often present. The solution in this case is to rid the building of such pests and ensure that others cannot get in.

Every possible cause must be examined and eliminated before coming to the conclusion that the

Do not handle the newly born young or disturb the nest. Gerbils are known to react to this intrusion by eating the young.

In this photo note that the nesting material which these fully furred young no longer need has already been removed. Although gerbils have clean habits, it is best to remove anything which can attract vermin. Since the cage has more occupants now, the bedding should also be changed more often. Photo by D.G. Robinson, Jr.

female is unsuitable to rear further litters. When this has been ascertained, she should be culled.

VERMIN

Vermin include here all types of mice, rats, insects and in fact any kind of living thing which is detrimental to the welfare of gerbils.

Mice are perhaps the most commonly encountered where the rearing of animals is concerned. The damage they do is not all that obvious at first, but in the long term their effects are radical. Mice will breed *very* quickly if left to settle for any period of time. They are verminous in that they carry all kinds of diseases which can be transmitted to gerbils. These diseases are passed on in their droppings and whenever they come into close contact with other animals. All storage containers for food should therefore be made from a non-chewable material that has a tight-fitting lid. It does not matter where a container is placed; the mice will find it. And if they can feed in it, they will contaminate the contents to such an extent that they are no longer safe for your gerbils. During the night also, the mice will run all over the gerbil's cages and frighten the occupants so much that the females will be likely to destroy their young.

Rats are even more dangerous. They will not only pass on diseases to gerbils but also some that are transmittable to man—and these can be fatal to humans! A rat will kill gerbils if it can gain entry to an insecure cage. To rid the gerbil establishment of such vermin is not an easy task once the mice or rats have gained a hold. Poison is perhaps the safest way—as long as it is laid well out of the reach of other animals and children, of course. There are many commercial rat and mouse poisons on the market; the instructions on the label should be followed to the letter.

EUTHANASIA

Euthanasia is another word for painless killing or, as it is sometimes termed, culling. The subject can be rather delicate and many used to feel that the subject should not be discussed with younger people. However, times come when it has to be used.

Gerbils that become seriously ill or injured beyond the limits of satisfactory recovery should be put to sleep in order to save them from further suffering. A seriously afflicted gerbil is a distressing sight to any animal lover, no matter what their views on euthanasia may be. Most animal organizations will put to sleep painlessly a gerbil that is beyond recovery. This service saves the gerbil owner much anxiety and, in economic terms, the cost is very low. A number of substances exist also that can be used to destroy gerbils painlessly. They should be used in extreme circumstances only—and certainly with some kind of supervision from an accepted authority.

The practice of killing gerbils by violent means is to be condemned out of hand. Not only because it is against the law in many areas to cause any animal pain and suffering, but it requires special knowledge to do the job cleanly and properly. Therefore, consult a vet or animal welfare society should you have to decide that any gerbil would be better off if it were destroyed.

Exhibition Gerbils

The gerbil fancy caters almost exclusively to the Mongolian gerbil. There are shows which include classes for other species of gerbil, but they do not often happen. In England, any animal that will produce a mutation is provided with a show standard and shows are promoted in order that the standard of excellence can be maintained. The gerbil fancy was started around 1968 when a handful of interested persons in England formed the National Mongolian Gerbil Society. At this time there was only the normal or Agouti-colored gerbil and the white or, as it was referred to at the time, the albino gerbil.

The white gerbil caused quite some concern among many fanciers because of the term albino that was attached to it. Any animal that is completely albino does not show any other colored hairs or markings. The Mongolian gerbil is different in this respect, the young white gerbil appearing to be completely white only until it reaches three months of age. At this age brown hairs start to grow on the top ridge of the tail; they do not cover the entire tail but are more prominent along the ridge. Because the Mongolian gerbil has these dark hairs, it has been suggested that it is in fact a Himalayan albino. The Himalayan albino is an incomplete albino, and good specimens show some coloring on the ears, nose, feet and tail. The eye of the Himalayan albino is slightly darker than that of the complete albino, which is a definite pink.

It was at first thought that the white gerbil would

Managing a white gerbil is not any different from an agouti gerbil, except for trying to keep the light fur from getting stained; avoid using newspaper or peat for nesting material. Photos by Studio Morgan.

help to produce a broken or spotted gerbil. The idea was to cross the white gerbil with a new mutation that had appeared at this time in the form of the white-spot gerbil. The mutation was reputedly supposed to have been discovered in Canada and was termed the "Canadian white-spot gerbil." This new type of color was imported into England, but it at first proved to be very difficult to breed from. The last two pairs were obtained by a serious gerbil breeder who mated a white gerbil to one of the new white-spot females. This proved to be a success, but it did not improve the areas of white in the spotting. The appearance of more young white-spots certainly halted its decline in numbers and possibly saved the mutant from extinction. The fault with these new young white-spots was that they contained too much of the factor for white, and therefore the Agouti pattern was much too light. By breeding back to the Agouti line the normal dark Agouti was reestablished.

Since those early days of gerbil breeding the colors have changed very little; the white-spot is in the hands of only a few experienced breeders, and the white, although more widespread than it was, is still a rarity. No doubt with more intensive breeding other gerbil mutations will appear. As detailed earlier, there are examples of black and silver gerbils, so it is quite possible that the gerbil fancy will grow to its full potential after all.

In England there are in existence standards to which gerbils are exhibited. These standards are based on what it is thought the perfect gerbil should look like. The wild gerbil will be far removed from this description because certain points in the exhibition gerbil are enhanced in order to improve the gerbil's overall appearance.

There, are, however, criticisms of this type of selective breeding. In dogs the extent of selective breeding has resulted in some remarkable changes in the shape and character of the species. It is said by some that the temperament of the animal is severely affected with the result that nervousness is an inherited feature. This has never been proved to be the case with gerbils even though they can be inbred quite intensively.

Below are reproduced the English exhibition standards as laid down by the National Mongolian Gerbil Society. They are the first standards and therefore will be subject to later amendments that may be thought to be required to improve the exhibition gerbil.

THE NORMAL AGOUTI

The top color shall be soft golden red, evenly covered with back ticking over the back and sides, carried well down to a dark grey at the roots. The belly fur shall be as white as possible. The underside of the tail shall be slightly lighter in color than that of the body. The top side of the tail only shall be the same as the body, ticked with black and showing a ridge the full length of the tail, shading to an almost black tuft. The ears shall be covered with fine light grey hair, bordered with a soft golden red free from ticking. The eyes shall be jet black and encircled with a distinctive light grey hair. The toenails shall be black.

ALBINO AGOUTI

The entire coat shall be pure white to the roots with no shading or markings whatever. The eyes shall be a clear pink in color. The ears shall be flesh colored, covered with fine white hair. The toe nails shall be neutral in color.

It will be noted that the white gerbil contravenes this standard because of the appearance of the colored hairs that grow on the tail as the animal reaches maturity.

WHITE-SPOT

The standard for the white-spot is the same as that for the normal Agouti except that allowance is made for the white markings. These should be clearly defined and as evenly distributed as possible on the nose, head, nape of neck, feet and tail.

THE STANDARD

The basic standard for all varieties of Mongolian gerbil is the same for all colors. That is to say that the basic shape is the same. The marks for the standard are as follows:

Type	20 points
Color	15 points
Fur	15 points
Condition	20 points
Size	15 points
Eyes	5 points
Ears	5 points
Tuft of Tail	5 points

Total . . . 100 points

Penalties to be deducted from the gerbil's total of points:

Disease or intractability	*Disqualification*
Sores or wounds	Minus 20 points maximum
Excess fat	10 points
Molting	10 points
Dirty or stained fur	10 points
Dirty show pens	5 points

Maximum of total of points to be lost—55 points

These standards are defined as follows:

Type: The body shall be moderately firm and plump—but not fat. The head shall be short and broad and set well into the body.

Condition: The Mongolian gerbil shall be very alert at all times and easily handled. The fur should have a healthy sheen and not be molting.

Fur: The fur shall be thick, as short as possible and soft to the touch. Attention should be paid to the belly fur which shall be as dense as possible.

Size: The Mongolian gerbil shall be as large as possible. The tail shall be the same length as the body when fully adult. The length of the tail will be judged in relation to the age of the gerbil. The female's size (which is smaller than the male) will be taken into consideration in mixed classes.

Eyes: The eyes shall be large (not bulging), widely set and bright.

Ears: The ears shall be fairly small, not too rounded and carried erect.

The way this standard is interpreted is entirely up to the judge's own discretion.

The Mongolian gerbil is shown in a special show pen designed in such a way that the gerbil is exhibited to its best advantage. The pen or cage is small, light in weight and easily maintained. These pens can be purchased ready-made, or you can make them.

Plywood of ¼" thickness is used throughout the whole construction. Cut the base first; it measures 8 inches by 6 inches. Then cut the back, which is 8½ inches by 6 inches. The sides are a little more difficult as they should be cut to allow for the sloping front of the pen. First, cut out a piece of timber 6 inches square; mark one edge as the top and one edge as the front side. It does not matter which you choose, so long as the cleanest side of the plywood is on the outside when the pen is put together. Along the top edge, measure 2 inches and mark it; similarly along the front edge, measure 2 inches from where the bottom of the pen will be and mark it as before. With a ruler, draw a straight line be-

An excellent male gerbil specimen, although its tail is perhaps a tri-fle shorter than what the ideal male gerbil would have. Photo by D.G. Robinson, Jr.

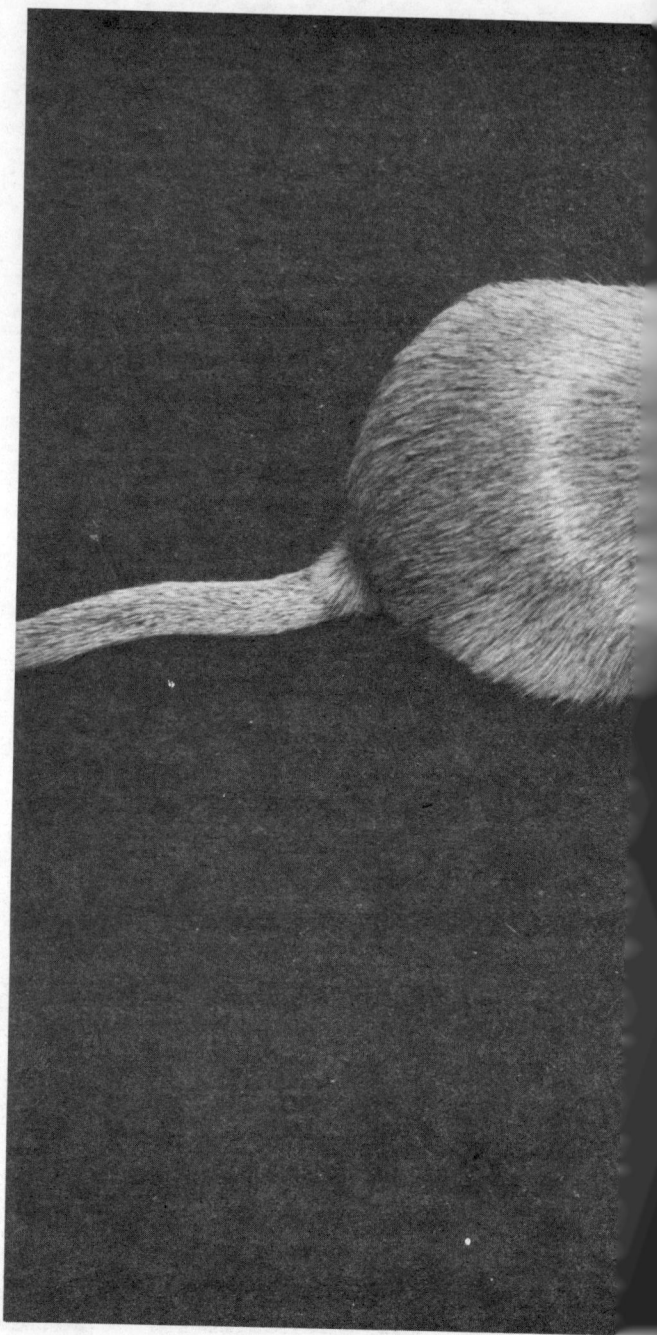

Dorsal view of adult Mongolian gerbils. Standards for a male and female gerbil with respect to size are slightly different. The female (right) is generally smaller than the male (left). Photo by D. G. Robinson, Jr.

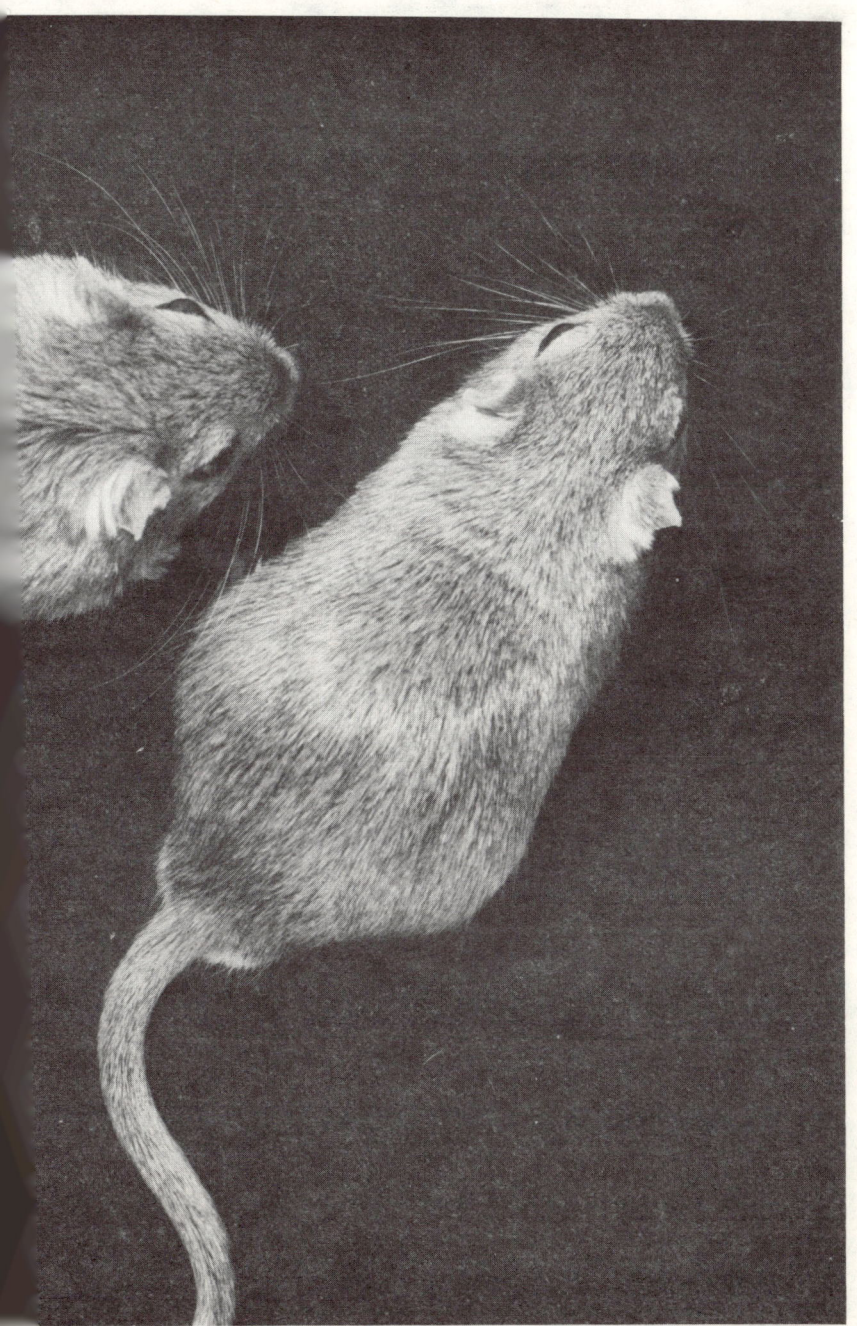

An exhibition or show cage for gerbils. Photo by Studio Morgan.

tween the two marks running diagonally across the timber. Saw along this line and discard the top piece which is now waste. Cut two of these sides but be sure that they are opposites and face the same way when put together.

The back, base and two sides can now be tacked together with ¾ inch panel pins. This is not very difficult if you do it calmly! To help bond the edges together, use a white wood glue. Smear a thin film along both of the edges you are handling and after the glue has become tacky press the pieces together and drive in the panel pins. Don't be worried if the glue runs down the sides of the timber, since it can be removed later when it has set. While the half-constructed pen is drying, cut from the remaining plywood a piece measuring 8 inches by 1¾ inches for the top and another of the same measurements for the front of the

An adequate—although not a too appealing—show cage. Photo by Morgan Studio.

pen. When the rest of the pen has dried and the glue is hard, the top and front can be tacked into place using the glue as before.

The wire front of the pen is very difficult to make if one has not had experience with this type of work before. It is made from plated wire and punch bar. There are 14 cross wires placed 3/8 inch apart. They are pushed through the punch bar holes and soldered into position. The punch bar will now measure 5 inches in length and will accommodate as stated 14 wires. The wire front can be made on a jig if required.

To make the hinges, there are two alternatives: the wire at the bottom of the pen front can be cut ½ inch longer than the rest at each end, which will make the wire 9 inches long. When the pen is cut out as described before, it should not be glued together but left until the wire front is made. The reason for this is that the two sides are drilled at each side to allow the bottom wire to be passed through and then bent flat. The wire front will now hinge and the rest of the pen is put together as before.

The other alternative is to cut two pieces of punch-bar 2 inches long. These are then threaded onto the bottom wire before it is soldered into position. The hinges are then tacked onto the inside of the two sides. The pen is now almost completed except for the addition of the catch and handle. The catch is made from two pieces of the wire that are used in the construction of the wire front. Cut one of them 2 inches long and bend it at an angle of 45 degrees. Place it on the topmost wire of the front and bend the ends around this wire. The other half of the catch requires a small hole drilled in the top of the pen. This piece should be cut 1½ inches long and also bent at an angle of 45 degrees. It should be noted that this wire should be bent at a point two-thirds of the way along its length; this is to say that from the angle to the other end, ½ inch long. The long end is then passed through the hole in the top of the pen from underneath, and the end that protrudes is bent into a small loop and then tapped flat. When the wire front is closed, the catch on top of the pen comes into position in the center of the other half of the catch on the front, and it can then be securely fastened.

The final stages include the protection of all expos-ed edges and the painting of the finished product. To cover the edges that can be chewed by the gerbil, cut a piece of thin tin the length of the edge it is intended for and half an inch wide. Tack the tin along the edge with ½ inch pins, bend it around the edge and do the same on that side. Be sure to file flat any nails that come through as they can cause serious injury to both you and the gerbil if they are left protruding.

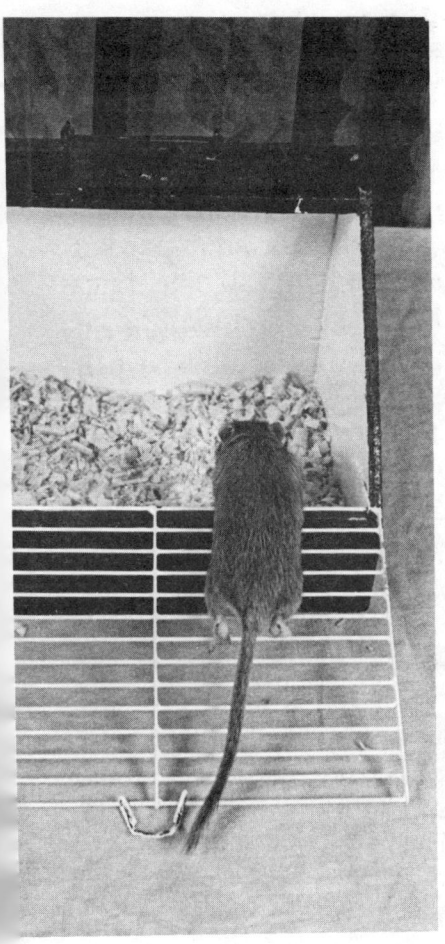

When a gerbil is already used to the confines of a Maxey cage, it will get into it without being prompted, especially if some food is placed in the cage.

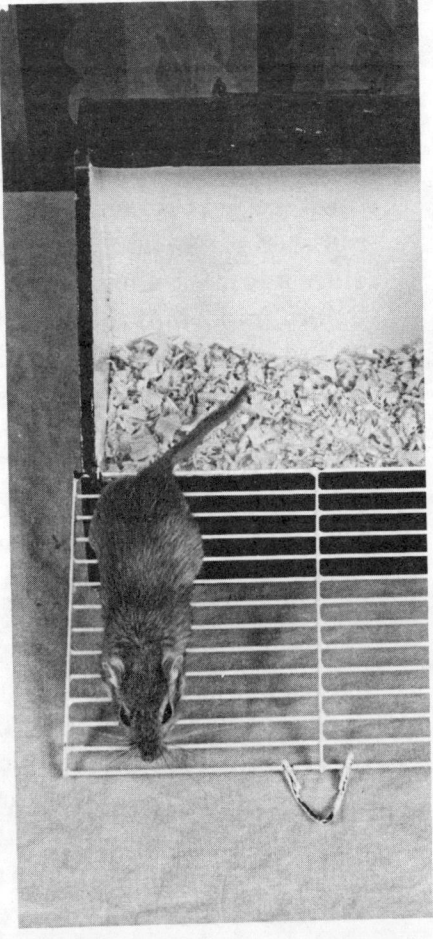

Running after and catching a loose gerbil in the room is hard work, so it will be best to secure the lid of the Maxey cage as soon as the animal is inside. Photos by Morgan Studio.

213

Nowadays few paints on the market contain lead; those that do usually bear a label that states the fact. Avoid lead paint, of course, in painting the cage. The whole of the inside and outside of the pen can now be primed with an ordinary undercoat paint. Latex-base paint is also quite satisfactory for this purpose and has the advantage that it dries quickly. A second coat is required to fill any rough grain in the timber. The final coat will be full gloss paint; to obtain a really good finish, two coats of this are recommended. The pen should be painted brilliant white on all inside surfaces and the whole of the wire front. The exterior is best black all over.

Unless the exhibitor has his own transport, the sending of his stock to shows can be a difficult problem. A box can be constructed, however, to take as many show pens as is comfortable for one person to carry. A number of designs are possible, but whichever one is chosen it must allow a free circulation of fresh air. This is very important if the exhibits are to arrive at the show in the best condition possible. Gerbils perspire a great deal in cramped conditions and ruin the appearance of their coats. Hence, without the right equipment all your work and trouble in preparing exhibits for the show can become a complete waste of time.

Choosing gerbils for showing is largely a matter of experience. As the time for the show approaches, take a look at the available stock and note those that are already in good condition and those that are reaching good condition. The difficulty with those that are in good condition is that they can suddenly "go over the top" and decline in condition right at the most important time, on the day of the show. The ones that are reaching good condition should continue to improve with care, so you are more or less assured that they will be right on the day of the show.

A carrying case with handles ensure the safe transport of gerbils to the show place. Photo by Studio Morgan.

Good condition can be maintained by the addition of small seeds to the diet. Linseed is very good as it contains a large amount of oil which gives the coat an added luster. Those gerbils which are reaching good condition should be fed as usual, with the addition of a very small amount of seeds. Too much will bring on the desired condition too early, thus spoiling the chances of steadily improving its condition right up to the day of the show.

For show purposes the pen should have a covering a clean sawdust about ½ an inch deep on the floor, but if the gerbils have to travel by rail it is advisable to place a handful of hay in with the gerbil in which it can sleep. If the box has to spend the night in a cold atmosphere, the hay will help keep the gerbil warm and provide it with some kind of security. A small amount of food can also be included, along with a little bit of raw potato or carrot. The vegetable provides the gerbil with a source of moisture, as the inclusion of water would be impossible under such circumstances. The stewards at the show will remove any additions before your exhibit is placed before the judge; they will usually replace them before your box is sent back to you.

When you first became interested in gerbils you probably went to a reputable pet shop in the neighborhood. The dealer sold you, at a moderate price, healthy animals with which you began gerbiling. Later he gave you much-needed advice whenever you asked, and supplied you with the things necessary to raise hearty, happy pets. But now you're thinking about entering your gerbils in competition. Your pet dealer has acquainted you with breeders who specialize in raising exhibition-quality animals. Contact one or several of these persons who have shown his or her gerbils and has won some awards. You can then be assured of getting animals that have been bred from his own stock: there is thus every chance that they will produce litters that are just as good. No exhibitor of livestock sells his very best, of course, unless he is giving up or for some reason he is forced to reduce his stock. It is a good idea to try to obtain a young trio of two females and one male that have been kept together. The advantage here is that the male can be shown while the females are rearing their litters of young. Be quite ruthless in selecting only the best from any litter that is bred. Failure in this respect will only result in a decline in the good type of your stock.

Another advantage of buying a trio is that a pair of young or even three of them can be held and mated back to their respective parent according to their sex. This principle is inbreeding; it fixes in the stock all of the

Each show cage is intended to house only one gerbil for showing. A small amount of food can keep it content during transport. Photo by Studio Morgan.

desirable good points that are required in the exhibition gerbil. Its use must be strictly controlled because it can just as easily fix the bad points. When trying to match exhibition gerbils, there are certain points that must be taken into consideration. Firstly, the good quality of the stock is of prime importance and must be maintained at all costs. Choose a male that has as many good qualities as possible and mate him to a female that has just as many good qualities but has yet one more that the male may be lacking in. This also can be applied vice versa. The aim here is to breed a gerbil that is better in most respects than either of its parents and so lifts the general standard of excellence.

Other qualities must also be taken into consideration as well as the general appearance of the gerbils. Good motherhood is very important for the general well-being of the entire stock. Bad mothers are notorious for passing this trait on to their daughters with the result that it becomes very difficult to rear litters at all. Gerbil females that prove to be useless at rearing their litters of young should be discarded without mercy. That is to say that they may be good exhibition animals, but if they will not rear a litter, the good line of excellence will suffer in the long run. The only alternative would be to try and foster their young onto another female, but here again the fancier is only deceiving himself because the young that are fostered will have to be bred from at some future time, and it could be that they follow in their mother's footsteps and also prove quite useless at rearing their own young.

Further Reading

Allen, G.M. 1940. *Natural History of Central Asia: The Mammals of China and Mongolia*. American Museum of Natural History, New York.

Barfield, M.A. and E.A. Beeman. 1968. "The oestrus cycle of the Mongolian gerbil," *J. of Reproduction and Fertility*.

Bentley-Aistrop, J. 1968. *The Mongolian Gerbil*. Dobson Books, London.

Davidson, R. 1960. *Introducing the Gerbil as a New Test Animal*. American Cyanamid Co.

Ellerman, J.R. 1940. *The Families and Genera of Living Rodents*, Vol. I. British Museum (Natural History), London.

Marston, J.H. and M.C. Chang. 1965. "The breeding, management, and reproductive physiology of the Mongolian gerbil," *Laboratory Animal Care*. 15(1).

Mossesson, G.R. and S. Scher. 1972. *Guinea Pigs and Other Laboratory Animals*. T.F.H. Publications, Neptune, N.J.

Robinson, D.G., Jr. 1967. *How to Raise and Train Gerbils*. T.F.H. Publications, Neptune, N.J.

Schwenther, V. 1957. "The need for new laboratory animals," *U.F.A.W. Handbook*, ed. 2, London.

_____. 1963. "The gerbil—a new laboratory animal," *Illinois Veterinarian*, 6.

Thornton, P.L. 1969. *All About Gerbils*. T.F.H. Publications, Neptune, N.J.

Walker, E.P. 1975. *Mammals of the World*. Ed. 3. John Hopkins Univ. Press, Baltimore.

Walters, J., P.J. Rogers, and J.U. Rogers. 1963. "The gerbil—a new subject in behavioral research," *Physiological Reports*, 12.

Woodcock, W.H. 1955. *Management and Breeding of a New Laboratory Species (Meriones libycus)*. Animal Technicians Association.

Index

Page numbers set in *italic* type refer to illustrations.

Fits 194-5
Fleas *187*, 189
Food 18, 39-40 (wild), 62, 102, *102*, 103-5, *105*, 106, *107*, 108-10, *108*, *111*, 112, *112*, 113, *113*, *142*, *144*, *145*, *146*, *171*, *178*; Tidbits *116*, 117
Forest Spiny Pocket Mice *(Heteromys)* 33-4

G
Genetics 150-1, 154-5, *155*, 158, *158*, 166
See Also Mutations
Gerbillus (Pigmy or Dwarf Gerbil) 10, *76*
Giant Rice Rat 18
Golden Gerbil *137*
Great Gerbil 11
Greater Egyptian Jerboa *(Allactaga)* 22
Guinea Pigs *163*
    Abyssinian *69*
    Agouti *68*
    Crested *69*

H
Hamsters 132, 168
    Albino *32*
    Banded Cinnamon *65*
Handling *57*, 61, *61*, 62, *63*, 64, *85*, *88*, *89*, *92*, 192, *194*
Harvest Mouse 16, *17*
Head 37-8
Heteromyidae ("Different Mice") 18-19, 26-7, 30-1, 33-5
Heteromys (Forest Spiny Pocket Mice) 33-4
Hibernation 36-7

Himalayan Albino Gerbil *162*, 163-4, 201
House Mice *20*

I
Inbreeding 167, 170, 172, 216-17
Injuries 192-4

J
Jaculus (Desert or Hairy-footed Jerboa) 22
Jerboas (Dipodidae) 18-19, 22-3
Jerusalem Gerbil 40

K
Kangaroo Mice *(Microdipodops)* 35
Kangaroo Rats *(Dipodomys)* 26, *27*, 30-1
Kenya Mole Rat *9*
King Gerbil *(Tatera Boehmi)* 13

L
Lemmings *(Lemmus)* 18
Lemmus (Lemmings) 18
Lemmus Lemmus (Norway Lemming) 18
Libyan Gerbil 40, 173
Lice 189, 191
Lifespan 41
Liomys (Spiny Pocket Mice) 33-5

M
Mange 183-6, *183*
Maxey Cage *See* Show Pen
Meriones unguiculatus (Mongolian Gerbil) *4*, *5*, 10, 36, 40, *42*, 43-52, *151*, *157*, 208-9